GREETINGS FROM
NEW JERSEY

To Bee Marie Turd—

A Jersey Gal from the
get go!

Helen O'Rake
12/15/02
Spring Lake

Greetings from NEW JERSEY

© CURT TEICH & CO., INC.

GREETINGS FROM NEW JERSEY

A Postcard Tour of the Garden State

Helen-Chantal Pike

Rutgers University Press • New Brunswick, New Jersey

1

Designed by Curt Teich & Company, Inc., Chicago,
this postcard was distributed by Lynn B. Boyer Jr. of Wildwood.
Can you guess which historic landmarks were used to fill out the letters?

Library of Congress Cataloging-in-Publication Data

Pike, Helen C.
    Greetings from New Jersey : a postcard tour of the Garden State / Helen-Chantal Pike.
        p.   cm.
    Includes index.
    ISBN 0-8135-2997-2 (alk. paper)
        1. New Jersey—History, Local—Pictorial works.   2. New Jersey—History—20th century—
    Pictorial works.   3. New Jersey—Social life and customs—20th century—Pictorial works.
    4. Postcards—New Jersey.   I. Title.

F135.P55 2001
974.9'043—dc21
                                                                                                    2001019297

British Cataloging-in-Publication data for this book is available from the British Library.

Designed and typeset by Ellen C. Dawson

Manufactured in China

This book is dedicated to the memory of my mother,
Helene Fernande Chapon Pike,
a Parisian who loved telling people she was from New Jersey.

2
Circa 1900.

Contents

Acknowledgments

The footsteps for *Greetings from New Jersey* took me many places and often in the company of individuals who love living here. For the unabashed affection for their adopted state I want to thank the Barrie sisters from Queens, New York; Arlene Heyson and Muriel Tiedeman, who enthusiastically kept telling me about places I had never been to; Barbara Tomlinson, teacher, mentor, friend; Glenn D. Vogel, who showed me how the postcards of my childhood could tell me stories; Cheryl Stoeber-Goff, artist and archivist, who reminded me I am a Jersey Girl at heart; Cathy Cohen and Julie Gannon, who made me use my name; and my fellow writers Pam Waterman, Mary Fowler, and Karen Plunkett-Powell for all of your support along the way. Thank you Anita Sawyer, Stella Young, Walter Hatch, Steve Gross, Doris Tice, Frank M. Culloo, and Clarence H. Still Jr.

I would also like to toss a bouquet to Mark Chapman of the *Boston Herald,* the only travel editor in North America to buy all the articles I ever wrote about my home state. Thank you for the steady paycheck; the Atlantic City chapter is for you. Thanks to Kristin McKeon at *New Jersey Monthly,* where this book had its genesis; Ellen Carroll, who sent me to some pretty interesting places in Asbury Park and Neptune for "The Coaster"; Jon Blackwell, who shared with me his Trentonian stories even while he worked at the *Asbury Park Press;* Jerseyean Andy Levine at Development Counsellors International, New York; Janet C. Wolf of the National Park Service, who toured me through beautiful South Jersey; and Eugene Dilbeck, director of the state's Division of Travel and Tourism when I came home in 1991. Thank you Rutgers University Press for making such a tempting package out of all this eye candy. A special thanks to Robert Burchfield who did the tour from Iowa, offering a fresh perspective as he went.

What else I know about New Jersey is due to the passion of the following people: Bob Ruffalo at Princeton Antiques Bookshop, Atlantic City; Marty Kane at the Lake Hopatcong Historical Museum; John DePalma of the Hoboken Historical Society; Edward Smyk, Passaic County historian; my dear friends Lorenzo Harris Jr., Peter Lucia, Evelyn Stryker Lewis, Rosemary Kelly Zimmerman, and Joan McLaughlin Flatley; Virginia Faulkner and Chris Wolff of the Garden State Postcard Club; and my three musketeers: Moe Cuocci, Barbara Booz, and John Rhody. *Un grand merci à Leslie Rhody, pour l'alimentation et l'amitié.*

I also want to thank Donna B. and John Zorn for their unfailing support, and E. Ashby Jones III, a fellow writer who helped float my boat. Newark is yours.

Greetings from New Jersey would not have been possible without all of you.

x

3
Postmarked 1912.

GREETINGS FROM
NEW JERSEY

Wish You Were Here

INTRODUCTION

Long before rock musician Bruce Springsteen picked up a glossy Tichnor Brothers postcard to decorate his first album cover in 1973, vacationers were sending the signature "Greetings from Asbury Park N.J." card to family and friends. They were also sending greetings from Newark, Camden, Sea Isle City, and Seaside Heights. In fact, sending postcards began as a fad in the final years of the nineteenth century as travel-happy Americans began scribbling their sentiments on thin, three-and-a-half-by-five-and-a-quarter-inch pieces of cardboard whose front sides were printed with a local view.

In the years following the end of the Civil War, middle-class travel in America boomed. Union soldiers returning to visit battle scenes in Pennsylvania, Maryland, and Virginia paused with their families for a night, or two, in New Jersey. As America's Industrial Revolution picked up steam, health resorts along the seacoast and in the state's forested hideaways opened up, offering fresh air and saltwater as cures for those working and living in the cities. At the same time, prosperous European travelers, their curiosity finally piqued by the stories of Washington Irving, Mark Twain, and New Jersey's own James Fenimore Cooper, decided to come to America and see for themselves what brave new world had been tamed by the descendents of Puritans and fashioned by the continental émigrés. Steamships landed them on the Hudson River, and trains took them to destinations in the former colony that was number eleven out of the original thirteen. During this same period, African Americans freed from slavery in the South traveled north to settle in such New Jersey towns as Lawnside, Whitesboro, Medford, New Brunswick, East Orange, Montclair, and Hackensack.

Like the indigenous Lenape and Algonquin nations, visitors to New Jersey were nomads. At times they even followed native footsteps to destinations named after the state's original inhabitants: Musconetcong, Assunpink, Watchung, Topenemus, Wickatunk, Metuchen, Rancocas, Manasquan, and Absegami Island. City residents from New York and Philadelphia also found their way to the Garden State, seeing with their own eyes the rolling hills and valleys, the open countryside, and the waters that supplied their metropolitan larders with fruits, vegetables, dairy products, meat, poultry, and fish.

Vacationers weren't the only travelers. Photographers loaded up their tripods and large-format cameras and journeyed to the mountains, the lakes, the cities, the seashores—wherever there was opportunity to photograph a scenic view and the tourists who were there. They set up studios, taking souvenir snapshots and printing them on heavy paper stock that could be sent more cheaply than letters through the mail. Vacationers who didn't yet own the new hand-held cameras just coming onto the market bought the flat cards, scrawled a simple salutation to satisfy the social mores of the day, licked a stamp, and sent them out. Lake Hopatcong photographer and self-proclaimed "Post Card Man" William J. Harris noted on his letterhead, "The time to take the picture is when you see it. The historic value of things, fixed in the form of a picture, is beyond price."

Everywhere the tourist went in New Jersey, postcards were sure to be there. A panoramic vista. The town square. A Civil War or American Revolutionary War monument. The hotels. A house of worship. Local humor. Trolleys. A covered bridge. The ferries. A railroad station. Those new-fangled automobiles. A restaurant. The amusement park. Main Street, New Jersey.

In 1893, when the first souvenir postcards were sent from the World's Columbian Exposition in Chicago, the telephone was not yet commonplace, let alone affordable. Postcards were an inexpensive way for people to let a relative know they would be arriving on the evening train; to order a load of coal for the winter; to inquire about the health of a friend. In 1896 you could buy and send a postcard for two copper coins—a penny for the card and one for the postage. With twice-a-day mail delivery, you could invite friends to tea that morning and expect to see them that afternoon.

Arthur Livingston of New York began printing souvenir black-and-white postcards with the "Greetings from . . . " salutation in 1898. He started with New York views, the "Greetings from" in separate script. Soon other metropolitan printers jumped on the bandwagon. Regional and local stationers issued their own cards, too. Businesses used postcards as direct-mail advertisements. Retail stores opened, selling nothing but postcards. Atlantic City and Asbury Park had boardwalk outlets. Photographers had studio props such as pickle barrels, a cutout of a canoe on the high seas, or bicycles set against a bird's-eye view backdrop creating the illusion that those being photographed for a souvenir card were riding over the resort. In the early years of the twentieth century postcard sending and collecting reached such a fevered pitch that popular magazines deemed the postcard phenomenon a craze. In 1908 the United States Post Office Department delivered a staggering 667,777,798 postcards.

The little cards solved a lot of communications problems, especially for those of few words or for those who didn't like writing letters. The post office helped the prose-shy by restricting the messages to the front of the cards in those early days. On the front of a card showing the lifesaving crew at practice in the Holly Beach section of Wildwood, the writer scrawled on the side of the overturned boat, "Alice can't be stopped." On the front of a Main Street view of Asbury Park showing Cook's Beehive Department Store, Bill wrote to his friends in the photo department at Prudential Life Insurance in Newark, "Come on in, the water is fine."

It wasn't until 1907 that postal patrons were allowed to pen their epistles on the back of the postcards, newly divided to allow for the separation of addressee from the message. One writer filled the entire half of a card, detailing in tiny, perfectly legible penmanship the ceremony dedicating the Billy Sunday Tabernacle on March 24, 1915, in Paterson. Another used the back and front for a word game.

Writers informed their friends and acquaintances of all kinds of news. One couple had themselves photographed in a wicker rolling chair in Atlantic City by way of announcing that they had just gotten hitched. From health spas came reassuring words. Admirers of the famous and dead toured cemeteries and sent word of their pilgrimages to fellow enthusiasts.

Still others sent the news of horrific events they had witnessed, such as the *Atlantic City Flyer* train wreck in Eatontown or the opera house block fire in Cranford. Disasters gave an added boost to tourism destinations, as when the *Morro Castle* burned off the shore of Asbury Park in 1934. Its hulking remains just ten feet from Convention Hall provided a much-needed draw as the Great Depression years wore on. Even after the cruise ship was towed away, the photo card was still a popular seller, giving visitors bragging rights to having been in Asbury Park, site of the disaster.

In the explosion of domestic travel after World War II, the relationship between tourism and postcards changed markedly. Chrome postcards, based on the latest in photographic and printing techniques, were churned out by the thousands by Curt Teich of Chicago, the Tichnors of Boston, and Thomas Dexter of West Nyack, New York. What defined these cards was Kodachrome, sixteen-millimeter color movie film adapted to four-by-five-inch sheet film by Eastman Kodak. But then the Rochester, New York, film and photographic paper giant applied the smaller-cheaper-faster principle to its cameras, spawning an ongoing interest in amateur photography that has changed why tourists buy postcards. Nonetheless, despite digital cameras that now give you pictures on demand, the desire to let everybody know you've been somewhere endures.

In the pages that follow, color and black-and-white postcards were culled from more than two thousand to show what has made us laugh, cry, rail, remember, and boast at having been somewhere in New Jersey. They are grouped according to the state's six tourism regions. In the spirit of "three of anything makes a collection," the final chapter is to help you figure out what to do if you have that third card.

4

New Jersey's most recognized postcard thanks to native son Bruce Springsteen. It was originally designed by the Tichnor Brothers, Boston, and distributed by the American Postcard Company of Brick Township, New Jersey.

5

Resorts were huge markets for the burgeoning field of photography. Who had time to sit indoors to have a portrait painted when on vacation?

A Typical Boardwalk Scene, Atlantic City, N. J.

Circa 1900 postcard made in Germany where printing techniques were perfected.
The twelve different languages attested to all the countries in which this card was sold.
All a distributor or retail store owner had to do was add the local angle on the front.

7 & 8

These are two in a series of hand-colored cards Ethel Brook had made in Germany to advertise her souvenir postcard store on a prominent retail street in Hoboken in the early twentieth century. The site today is occupied by a dry cleaners.

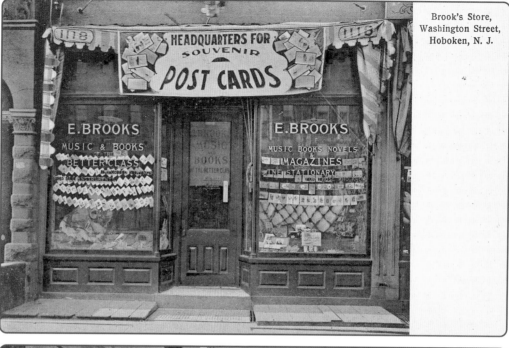

Brook's Store,
Washington Street,
Hoboken, N. J.

Brook's Store, Headquarters for Souvenir Post Cards, 1118 Washington St., Hoboken, N. J.

DEDICATION OF "THE BILLY SUNDAY TABERNACLE", MARCH 24TH, 1915.
PATERSON N.J.

9

In neatly cribbed handwriting, the sender recounts in detail the ceremony in honor of the one-time baseball slugger–turned–Bible thumper Billy Sunday, who is seated third from left on the podium.

Lotus Lilies, growing near Woodstown, New Jersey.

On Line of L.V.R.R. The Old Farmhouse at Bellewood.

10

Woodstown photographer E. W. Humphreys
took this picture. The print was hand-colored
and mass-produced in Germany and then
shipped back to Humphreys for resale.

11

To promote train travel, the Lehigh Valley Railroad
built an amusement park west of Pattenburg in Union Township.
The tourist destination opened the Fourth of July weekend 1904.
It closed in 1916.

Tomb of Walt Whitman, Harleigh Cemetery, Camden, N.J.

12

With their lushly landscaped grounds and elaborately carved tombs and monuments, cemeteries were popular Victorian-era destinations. This trend resulted in a spate of souvenir postcards. Poet Walt Whitman designed his tomb in Harleigh Cemetery in Camden in which he was buried in 1892.

The Jersey Central Flyer, Sandy Hook.

13

Railroad lines also had ferry connections to destinations. This early steamer to the Jersey shore landed in the sheltered harbor of Highlands across from the Sandy Hook peninsula.

14

Ferries also brought commuters across New Jersey's rivers as well as travelers looking to make a train connection for the various southern shore lines, as they did in Camden.

Ferry Boat between Philadelphia and Camden, N. J.

15

Mile one of the state's first train line from Perth Amboy to Camden was laid here in 1831. The locomotive was called the *John Bull*. In 1871 the Pennsylvania Railroad took over the operation, solidifying its control of the larger, and more lucrative, passenger and cargo route from Newark to Philadelphia.

JOHN BULL MONUMENT, MARKING FIRST RAILROAD IN NEW JERSEY, BORDENTOWN, N. J.

Flying High in Atlantic City, Having a Great Time Too Busy To Write.

THE FAULTS OF OUR
BROTHERS WE WRITE
ON THE SAND
THEIR VIRTUES UPON THE
TABLET OF LOVE AND
MEMORY.

HELLO BILL!

B.P.O.E.

Yours

THE SAND ARTIST AT WORK ON THE BEACH, ATLANTIC CITY, N. J.

The Elk Model in sand is an original idea of Frank B. Hubin. The modeling being done by James J. Taylor the originator of pictures in the sand. The photograph was taken by Adam Freund. This model of an Elk is acknowleged to be the finest sand picture ever made.

Postkarte = Carte Postale = Weltpostverein = Union postale universelle

Correspondenz-Karte = Levelezo-Lap = Dopisnice = Dopisnica = Post card = Karta korespondencyjna = Cartolina postale = Briefkaart = Carta Postala = Brefkort = Tarjeta postal = Korespondenoni listek = Cartao postal.

Affix
½d. Stamp

1d. Stamp
Foreign

Published by Frank B. Hubin's Big Post Card Store
813 Boardwalk, Atlantic City, N. J.
Copyright 1907

16
Atlantic City, site of numerous air meets, avidly promoted the new flying machines. This 1907 postcard also promotes Atlantic City's famous sand sculptors and the most influential fraternal organization of its time, the Benevolent and Protective Order of the Elks. It was sold at Hubin's Big Postcard Store on the boardwalk, where the owner, Frank, was an Elk.

17

How to get your roller skates to the newest Dreamland Arena? Take a bus! This postcard showed all the different lines to get a skater to "the world's largest unobstructed roller rink" at 985 Frelinghuysen Avenue in Newark.

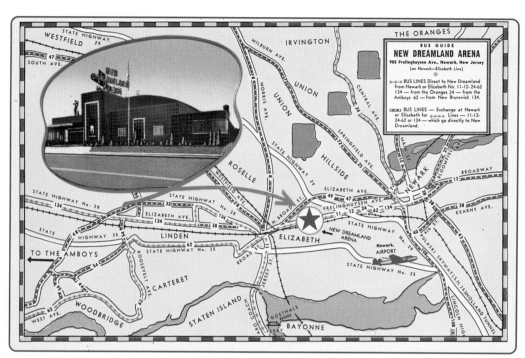

18

This Stickler photo card from Asbury Park shows the ill-fated cruise ship, S.S. *Morro Castle*, smoldering near Convention Hall. More than fourteen months after the tragedy, the postcard was still being sold and sent.

Passaic River Bridge underpassing the Pulaski Skyway, New Jersey Turnpike 4

Garden State Parkway Interchange near Woodbridge, New Jersey Turnpike

19 & 20
Construction of the New Jersey Turnpike began in 1948, the Garden State Parkway in 1952. Built over the Raritan and Passaic Rivers in 1932, the Pulaski Skyway ushered in the superhighway era. Here are two idyllic views after both roadways were completed.

21

Tichnor Brothers produced this soft-focused linen advertising postcard for a Cantonese family-style restaurant in Atlantic City.

22

Forgetful tourists have been known to send their stamped vacation cards in a bulk envelope to this post office with the request that they be sent postmarked from Wildwood.

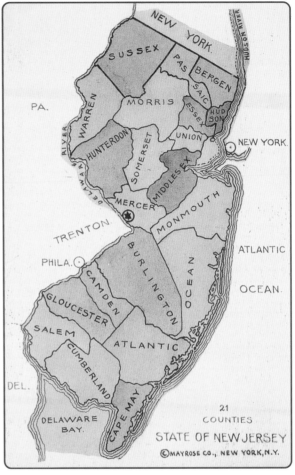

23
Novelty postcards are perennial favorites. This one is postmarked 1911.

24
The state's tourism regions were established
in the late 1980s by grouping various counties
together. Much earlier in the century
the Mayrose Company of New York
printed this handy postcard map.

Gone Day-Tripping

GATEWAY REGION

The date was October 28, 1886. The location was New York Harbor. The event was the formal acceptance of the Statue of Liberty.

Present that misty autumn day were New Jersey–born President Grover Cleveland and twenty-five hundred guests seated around the statue's base on Bedloe's Island. A flotilla of three hundred assorted civilian and military vessels filled with onlookers and musical bands crowded the harbor. Among the thousands who rimmed the various waterfronts were those in nearby Jersey City.

Had the mists lifted and the sun shone that day, what many would have seen was the symbol of freedom against the backdrop of promise that lay immediately in New Jersey. Westward behind the statue spread the open sky beckoning immigrants with unlimited opportunities, while to the north the spires of commerce in New York City held the advantages wealth could bring. But beyond the day's festivities, Lady Liberty overlooking the shipping channels stood for more than just a symbolic gateway to the United States. *Liberty Enlightening the World* helped define the moment when New Jersey was recognized internationally as a destination to which people would want to come.

By the 1880s New Yorkers had discovered the Garden State's northeast corridor as one ideal for day excursions. Stage, steam, and rail travel brought them to the verandas of Boynton Beach, the bucolic footpaths of Eagle Rock Reservation in the Watchung Range, the Great Falls in Paterson (much closer than Niagara), and the tranquil banks of the Saddle River. For picnics and amusements they went to the top of the Palisades or to Buster Brown's Castle in Bayonne. Hoboken's John Stevens, and later his sons, propelled travel with improvements in steam engines and the development of the first regular steam ferry service. Even inventor Thomas Alva Edison got caught up in the travel bug in an attempt to make rubber tires from the goldenrod plant.

In the Bergen Woods that lined the cliffs of Weehawken, the Palisades Amusement and Exhibition Company built Eldorado, a landscaped playground with a restaurant, dancing water fountains lit at night with colored lights, and a Moorish-style amphitheater with seating for eight thousand patrons. Here, lavish theater spectaculars with melodramatic names were staged. *King Solomon and the Destruction of Jerusalem; The Bombardment of Alexandria,* whose beating drums, cracking muskets, blaring trumpets, and thundering cannons reverberated on the Hudson; and *Egypt through the Centuries,* for which fifteen hundred ballet dancers were crammed on the stage. Ferried across at sunset, the evening revelers to Eldorado could look directly back across the river to the bright lights illuminating Forty-second Street in Manhattan's thriving theater district. Not far away was Highwood, Manhattan banker James King's country estate, where earlier in the century he entertained personal friend Daniel Webster, actress Fanny Kemble, and Mr. and Mrs. Charles Dickens on their first trip to America.

Farther south on the peninsula, excursion boats were daily leaving Jersey City for Rye Beach, New York; Bridgeport, Connecticut; and Rockaway, Queens. At the same time, the Pennsylvania Railroad Company was solidifying and expanding an impressive network of passenger, cargo, and ferry lines. In 1936 the jewel in its New Jersey railroad necklace was the new Pennsylvania Station in Newark. The terminal was a hub for five national trunk lines; its interior platforms were designed to handle four different passenger exchanges: street-level buses; aboveground and outbound commuter lines to the growing suburban towns;

inbound, underground electric lines that went to New York City; and platforms for continental rail travel.

Day-trippers eventually turned their desire for rest and relaxation into overnight journeys. So did others. New Englanders and Canadians came to New Jersey on their way to Washington, D.C., and sunnier climes. Southerners wanting to escape the crushing heat of their Low Country summers made their way north. Would-be ministers and scholars came here to go to school. Europeans wanting to see the Wild West landed in Hoboken to meet connecting trains. More than one family emigrated and stayed. In Rutherford, George and Charlotte Garraway of England settled with their young son, George. In 1902 George and his younger brother, Arthur, opened a stationery store in which they also sold cameras and photographic supplies. George then began dabbling in photography and the printing of postcards. The photography business grew. In 1908 the brothers incorporated their business as the Garraway Photo-Art Company and in 1910 changed the name to the Garraway Company. Magazine work and the growing mail-order trade became the company's main business. But Garraway continued to print postcards as a sideline until 1948. Studio photographer William Broadwell divided his time between Newark in the winter and Colesville in the summer, where he printed postcards for Sussex County's tourist trade. As camera equipment became less cumbersome, automobiles more numerous, and roadways more versatile than railways, photographers got around more.

In 1912 Carl Fisher, creator of the Indianapolis Motor Speedway and Miami Beach, came up with the idea of a coast-to-coast road that would be christened the Lincoln Highway. Its east coast terminus was Times Square. Its first Garden State stop was Jersey City. The Lincoln Highway's proponents included the Goodyear Tire Company, the Packard Motor Car Company, and Gulf Gas, which promoted auto travel with its sponsorship of a weekly thirty-minute radio soap opera on WNBC. By the late 1940s New Jersey was experiencing massive traffic tie-ups, and the east-west cross-state turnpike was designed to alleviate it. In the 1950s construction of the north-south Garden State Parkway followed.

In 1909, as flying fever began sweeping the country, airstrips and factories that were little more than garages started popping up along the peninsula between Newark Bay and the Hudson River, wherever there was a stretch of open—though not always flat—land. But Newark politicians were myopically focused on developing Newark Bay for shipping. So in 1927 when the United States Post Office Department found that it was taking too long to get mail to and from its central distribution plant in the congested city, the department moved its operations to Hadley Field, an airstrip in New Brunswick.

It wasn't long before city leaders, with some help from Washington, began hastily converting 420 acres of Passaic River salt marsh to woo back the postal service. The following year the postal department returned, and in 1929 delivery time from Newark to Manhattan was clocked at a breathless thirty-three minutes. The euphoria didn't last. Wall Street crashed, and the Great Depression settled in. The Post Office Department decided that the airplanes had to do more than just carry the mail. And so was born passenger service. The Newark runway had no competition: Floyd Bennett Field was in an inaccessible part of Brooklyn, and North Beach Airport would not be turned into La Guardia Airport until around World War II. In 1931, the first year of service, more than ninety thousand people flew in and out of Newark Airport.

But what if all the postal department wanted to do was just send mail? New York stamp collector F. W. Kessler thought he had the answer. Kessler organized the Rocket Airplane Corporation of America and hired Willy Ley to design a rocket plane fueled by liquid oxygen and alcohol that could shoot the mail across Greenwood Lake, from New York to New Jersey. On February 23, 1936, Ley tried to propel one hundred pounds of mail—six thousand postcards and letters—across the frozen expanse of Greenwood Lake. On his first attempt he used a catapult, which resulted in the rocket going straight up and then straight down. On the second attempt, a rocket was shot directly across the lake. But the sheer force of speed ripped the wings off, sending the projectile to the ice, mission unaccomplished.

Kessler and Ley's experiment didn't help the mail. It didn't stop it, either. Nor the tourists from sending Greenwood Lake postcards. In time, the area around the lake has become residential and the postcards of it as a day-tripping destination from Pompton Lakes and then as an overnight resort sought after.

Hudson, Bergen, Passaic, Essex, and Union are the Gateway counties.

Clipper passing Statue of Liberty   P A A Photo   80

Tice Tavern, Famous Coffee House of Revolutionary Times, Jersey City, N. J.

2132

25
President Grover Cleveland dedicated
Liberty Enlightening the World.
Placed at the mouth of the Hudson River,
with Jersey City as the backdrop,
the statue faces the Verrazano
Narrows between Manhattan and Staten Islands.
This dramatic photo was taken in the 1930s
shortly after commercial flights
started at Newark Airport.

26
Hospitality began at a tavern.
Westbound stagecoach travelers through Bergen Township
found respite at the intersection of what became
Bergen and Glenwood Avenues.
The original 1762 Eagle Tavern gave way to an establishment
built in 1815 by John Tise. It was torn down in the early twentieth century
as traffic patterns changed and travelers congregated
where several modes of transportation came together.

Pennsylvania Railroad Depot.   Jersey City, N. J.

27
New Jersey Railroad tracks
were cut through the Bergen Hill
neighborhood of Jersey City
in 1837 and a terminal built
on the Hudson River waterfront.
Trolleys brought commuters to the
ferries to get to work in Manhattan.
The rail line to Philadelphia opened
in 1841. In 1871 the Pennsylvania
Railroad took over. This site on
Exchange Place now caters to
leisure pursuits as a park named
after city historian J. Owen Grundy.
Commuters use a new ferry dock
located just to the south.

Entrance to Lincoln Park, Jersey City,   10
New Jersey, showing Lincoln Statue

28
In 1905 the Hudson County
Parks Commission relandscaped
287 acres of swamp on the east side
of the Hackensack River into
Lincoln Park. It put in eleven
baseball diamonds, six football
fields, eighteen tennis courts,
a swimming pool, a quarter-mile
track, sunken gardens, and a
fountain. The Lincoln Highway
began at Times Square, went south
through the Holland Tunnel,
west into Jersey City, and on to
Route 1 on the other side of the
Hackensack River as it made its way
to San Francisco.

30

29

An early-twentieth-century novelty card.

Regarded as the heart of Jersey City, Journal Square came into existence
in the 1930s when what is now called Kennedy Boulevard was built over the
railroad cuts that once divided the city's five different neighborhoods.
This inner-city hub reflects some of the changes in how leisure time is spent:
from left, the Hotel Plaza is senior citizens' housing; the ten-story
26 Journal Square remains an office building; the Hotel Holland, a one-time
boardinghouse, is giving way to a branch of Hudson County Community
College; the Trust Company of New Jersey is a different financial institution;
and Loew's Jersey Theater, the over-the-top mix of Italian and Spanish baroque
styles that at one time had seating for thirty-two hundred and
was saved from the wrecking ball, is undergoing restoration.

No. 15—Castle Point, Hoboken, N. J,   (Stevens Residence)

J. KOEHLER N.Y.

31
Lawyer John Stevens,
who laid out Hoboken,
turned to steam navigation
and built the first steamboat
to travel the Hudson in 1798,
the first one to venture on the
Atlantic, and in 1811 the first
steam ferry linking Hoboken
and New York. In 1825 he built
his first steam train on his
property overlooking the Hudson.

$10

HOBOKEN, N.
JUN 7
3 30 PM
1905

POST CARD

THIS SIDE IS FOR THE ADDRESS ONLY.
CONFORMS TO THE REQUIREMENTS OF SECTION 418 POSTAL
LAWS AND REGULATIONS.

31

PROC
JUN.
8
AM
1905
REC'D

Mrs Gustaf Weman

Box 146

Proctor Vt

32

The disastrous fire of 1900 wiped out the Hoboken piers.

FIRE BOAT, "ABRAM S. HEWITT" AT GREAT DOCK FIRE, HOBOKEN, N.J

F. O. Temme Co., Orange, N. J. Printed in Germany.

33

This artist's rendering shows that German steam-powered ships still had masts for sails in order to take advantage of wind power. The Hoboken piers were home ports for a wide variety of international cruise, freight, and ferry lines. In World War I, the government confiscated the Hamburg and North German Lloyd lines and until recently used their docks for domestic exports. This site today is Pier A Park.

The Hamburg-American Line Piers, Hoboken, N. J.

96-52

34
If you ever wondered what it must look like.

35
On the north side of Newark Street near River Street
since John Servanti opened its doors in 1899, this Hoboken
seafood restaurant, a block away from the pier, dates from the
days when this was a working-class neighborhood of European
immigrants, many of whom worked on the waterfront.
Restaurant patrons included visitors as well as residents.

36

At the southern edge of Eldorado was a Rhenish-style castle where visitors ate and drank. Karl Bitter added his studio to the castle's northern end. Bitter was known for the signature lions that graced the original Prudential Life Insurance Company headquarters building in Newark.

KARL BITTER'S STUDIO, ELDORADO. WEEHAWKEN, N.J.

Hamilton Monument, Hudson River and New York City in the distance, Weehawken, N. J.

1804   1894
UPON THIS STONE
RESTED THE HEAD
OF THE PATRIOT SOLDIER
ALEXANDER HAMILTON
AFTER THE DUEL WITH
AARON BURR
FOUGHT JULY 11TH
1804

37

One-time Elizabeth schoolmates Alexander Hamilton and Aaron Burr became bitter political foes when Hamilton thwarted Burr's efforts to become New York's governor. The resulting duel at James King's estate, July 11, 1804, left the nearsighted Hamilton mortally wounded, uttering the words, "I am a dead man." To which Burr replied, "He may thank me. I made him a great man."

38

A piece of New Jersey's car culture: the connection between the western tubes of the Lincoln Tunnel and the New Jersey Turnpike spur in Weehawken. In 1937 the south, or right, tunnel tube was finished at a cost of $35 million and fifteen lives. The tunnel's skeleton required fifty thousand tons of iron and steel fastened together with 346,000 bolts, each weighing ten pounds with nuts and washers.

THE TWIN STATE AND CAPITOL THEATRES, UNION CITY, N. J.

39

Religious theater in Union City competed with offerings at secular outlets, notably the twin State and Capitol Theatres that eventually became part of Keith's RKO movie chain.

CAPT. BALDWIN MAKING HIS FIRST FLIGHT IN ARLINGTON, N.J. MAY 25, 1909.

40

Noted balloonist Beven Baldwin, who later went on to design air strips for Philadelphia and Atlantic City, tried his hand at flying this early version of a fixed-wing aircraft.

The Palisades and Hudson River   Englewood, N. J.

41

Rising five hundred feet above the Hudson River, the Palisades offer breathtaking views and places to picnic. Until an alliance of the New Jersey Federation of Women's Clubs successfully halted blasting at the base of the cliffs at the end of the nineteenth century, Belgian blocks were being fashioned out of the basaltic rock as pavers to line New York City streets. When excavations began in 1926 for the George Washington Bridge, workers discovered dinosaur tracks dating from the Triassic period.

GEORGE WASHINGTON BRIDGE ENTRANCE AND TOLL BOOTHS IN N. J.

(Courtesy Port of New York Authority)

42
In 1931 the GWB, as the bridge is called in nightly broadcast traffic reports, was dedicated: $31 million of suspension engineering, $9 million in roadway approaches between Fort Lee and West 178th Street in Manhattan, and $15 million in real estate and interest, for a total of $55 million. By 1947 more than fourteen million vehicles were making their way over the bridge; twelve million were cars.

PALISADES
Amusement Park

43
"American's Greatest Amusement Value featuring 175 thrilling rides and attractions and eight giant colorful midways one mile south of the George Washington Bridge. World's Only Giant Wheel and Jungleland." New Jersey's most beloved pre–theme park sprawled across the red sandstone rock columns of Fort Lee and Cliffside Park from 1898 to 1971. In the mid-1960s the park's red, white, and blue motif was changed to various shades of greens, oranges, and yellows—colors that show well in chrome postcards.

Bridge, showing Post Office, River Edge, N. J.

Arcola Mill. - Ridgewood N. J.

44
This colorized advertising postcard not only alerted travelers
to Mr. Brown's grocery store but also to the post office that took care
of a number of rural delivery routes to surrounding communities.

45
This square fieldstone and shingled tower
on the bank of Saddle River was built in 1899
to mark the site of the historic Old Red Mill,
where blankets had been made
for the colonial troops.
At one time part of a private garden estate,
the property is one of the smaller parks
in the Bergen County system
and is located in Paramus.

BROWN'S GRAND VIEW LODGE
On the New Direct U. S. Route 202
Through the Picturesque Valley Road, Mahwah, N. J.
A Delightful Overnight Stop
Where Your Every Comfort Is Supplied
Varied Size Cabins
Tel. Cragmere 3835

46

Weary road travelers found respite here on the new U.S. Route 202 linking New England to Pennsylvania farther southwest in New Jersey at Lambertville. Through Mahwah, the highway shared the Valley Road, a three-mile stretch shaded by maples and dotted with pine trees and views overlooking the Ramapo River Valley. This way station at the New York State border had all the requisite signs to attract automobile tourists: gas, phone, food, and lodging.

Your order received, for which we thank you. Same will have our prompt attention.

Place your orders now for Bay Trees and Ornamental Evergreens.

We have probably the largest stock in the country.

BOBBINK & ATKINS

NURSERYMEN AND LANDSCAPE ARCHITECTS

RUTHERFORD, N. J.

SHIPPING BAY TREES IN SPRING

47

Horticulturist Lambertus Bobbink and salesperson Fred Atkins joined forces in 1898 and came to prominence supplying estates and private homes with the country's first two-year-old budded roses and ornamental shrubbery.

48

The 750-acre Meadowlands Sports Complex on former swamp and meadows created by the Hackensack River opened in 1976. Ten million people come here each year for horseracing, professional sports, and rock concerts.

49

Nine miles long, Greenwood Lake straddles part of West Milford Township in Passaic County in New Jersey and Greenwood Lake, New York. Though the lake is now rimmed by year-round homes, this original summer colony was made popular in 1875 by the Erie Railroad from Montclair. With the north-eastern shoreline as a backdrop, this motor-powered ice plane had a very brief run some time in the winter of 1960–61. Abercrombie Island, on the other hand, disengaged from the lake bottom and floated south and reattached itself—trees, rocks, shrub, soil—to the lake's eastern shore.

Factories along Passaic River

JOHN P. HOLLAND MONUMENT, PATERSON, N. J. SUBMARINE BOAT INVENTOR—CITIZEN OF PATERSON   37

4A-H528

50 & 51
In 1877 Irish émigré
John P. Holland used the
Passaic—the state's second
largest river—to test his submarine
design. Four vessels later,
he successfully designed one
for the U.S. Navy. His third sub,
Fenian Ram, was named for
the Irish independence group
that funded it. It stands in
West Side Park overlooking
the Passaic in Paterson.

52

John Ryle revolutionized the silk industry in 1840 when he came up with a way to wind silk on a spool. By the time of the 1914 Paterson Exposition, the decline in the silk industry was slowly under way due to the invention of rayon.

Paterson Silk Exposition 1914

Henry England Old ribbon weaver. Age 78.

Loom made near Coventry, England in 1765.

53

Located in the Garret Mountain Reservation, the crenellated fortress built by silk titan Catholina Lambert houses the Passaic County Park Commission and county museum, which holds the largest research archives of John P. Holland's groundbreaking work on submarine design.

Belle Vista Castle, Paterson, N.J.

Gone
Day-Tripping

35

Passaic Falls in Winter, Paterson. N.J.

63289

54

Treacherous no matter what the season, the Great Falls rises 104 feet above tidewater. In Paterson's early days, many people lost their lives picking their way along the edges just to see the dramatic drop. For some it was a cheaper vista than traveling all the way to Niagara Falls. Its presence has inspired everything from the poetry of William Carlos Williams to a scene of intimidation in the hit television show *The Sopranos*. The footbridge was opened on September 30, 1827, to much fanfare and the daredevil stunt of Sam Patch, a local cotton mill spinner, who jumped seventy feet from a rock overhanging the basin to the waters below and survived.

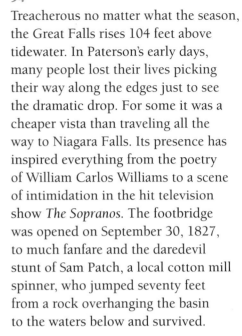
PUBLIC LIBRARY.

COURT HOUSE

GREETINGS

FROM NEWARK N.J.

63556

FIREMEN'S INSURANCE BUILDING.

NEW PRUDENTIAL (PUBLIC SERVICE) BUILDING.

55

This 1912 view shows some of Newark's more important civic and business addresses.

56

On part of the site now occupied by the New Jersey Performing Arts Center, the tubes were the earliest metropolitan subway system connecting Newark and Jersey City to New York on the Hudson & Manhattan Railroad Line in 1911.

New Park Place Station, Rapid Transit Line, New York to Newark, N. J.

P-63540

57

In 1916 investors erected the $1 million Robert Treat Hotel overlooking Military Park and named for the founder of Newark, who came here in 1666 from New Haven, Connecticut. The city's downtown was long overdue to have a high-rise hotel, and the Treat's opening was meant to coincide with the city's 250th anniversary celebration. President Woodrow Wilson and his wife were guests at the inaugural dinner sponsored by the Board of Trade. Recognized as a National Historic Site, the building's hotel rooms and Crystal Ballroom today share space with executive firms and the Newark television center for New Jersey Network. A modern hotel addition was constructed in 1991.

ROBERT TREAT HOTEL, NEWARK, N. J.   30780

Market Street from Broad St. Newark, N.

58

One of the world's busiest traffic intersections occurs where the east-west Market Street crosses Broad Street, Newark's north-south thoroughfare. It was a shopper's paradise as the concept of department stores took hold. Add an in-store restaurant and specialty services and you have ingredients that, mixed together differently fifty years later, created suburban shopping malls.

A Row of the „Finest" on Parade, Newark, N. J.

1308

Take your choose.

Rose.

59

Rose and her friend Theresa had lots of Newark's finest to choose from in this early-twentieth-century parade shot—except for those men with mustaches. The era's subtle social signals indicated that men with mustaches were already married.

FRIEDMAN'S MUSIC SHOP ～ *Everything for the Musician*

Expert Repairing on All Instruments. Prompt Service. The House That Made Newark Musical.

FRIEDMAN'S, 73 Springfield Avenue

2A552

Agents For

BUESCHER-ELKHART-HOLTON
Saxophones and Band Instruments

LUDWIG & LUDWIG
Drums

PARAMOUNT-VEGA-GIBSON-LUDWIG
Banjos

MARTIN & GIBSON
Mandolins & Guitars

ROTH & HEBELEIN
Violins & Bows

DEAGAN & LUDWIG
Xylophones, Bells, and Vibraphones

WILLIAMS & WALLACE ～ F. E. OLD'S
Trombones & Trumpets

Everything in
Teaching Books & Pieces - Standard
Make Radios - Sporting Goods
EASY PAYMENTS :: OPEN EVENINGS

MUSICAL INSTRUMENTS REPAIRED
Friedman's Music Shop
Telephone Market 2-7734
73 Springfield Avenue
NEWARK, NEW JERSEY

POST CARD

MADE BY CURT TEICH & CO., INC., CHICAGO, U.S.A.

PLACE ONE CENT STAMP HERE

60

With music halls came the
music stores to support Newark's
thriving music scene.

291:—MOSQUE THEATRE AND SALAAM TEMPLE, NEWARK, N. J.

61
Symphony Hall, built as
Salaam Temple in 1925,
was home to the New Jersey
Symphony Orchestra until 1997.
Plans are under way to incorporate
the theater into a cultural district
known as The Coast after an
African American entertainment
center in the city that thrived
in the late 1920s.

END OF A HEAT, WEEQUAHIC PARK TRACK, NEWARK, N.J.

62
Weequahic Park, built on the
original Waverly Fair Grounds
between Hillside and Elizabeth,
is enjoying a comeback,
though it doesn't include a
trotters' track for horses.

JULIAN ELTINGE
IN THE
"FASCINATING
WIDOW"

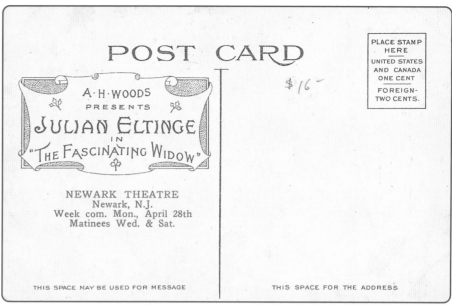

POST CARD

PLACE STAMP
HERE
UNITED STATES
AND CANADA
ONE CENT
FOREIGN-
TWO CENTS.

A·H·WOODS
PRESENTS
JULIAN ELTINGE
IN
"THE FASCINATING WIDOW"

NEWARK THEATRE
Newark, N.J.
Week com. Mon., April 28th
Matinees Wed. & Sat.

$16

THIS SPACE MAY BE USED FOR MESSAGE   THIS SPACE FOR THE ADDRESS

Newark Theatre.   Newark, N.J.

63 & 64

Leisure pursuits have always included theater entertainment of one kind or another.
The Newark Theatre was located at 167 Market Street, and postcards were early on used as direct-mail promotions.

Ballantine's Gate-way, Newark, N. J.

Bird's-eye View Branch Brook Park, Newark, N.J.

65 & 66

The oldest county park system
in the country began in Newark
when the Essex County Recreation
Commission was established
in 1895. Two miles in length,
the park incorporated thirty acres
of Robert Ballentine's estate,
including his gatehouses, which
he subsequently donated.
The French renaissance gatehouses
were designed by society architects
Carrère & Hastings of New York.
The Olmsted brothers designed
the sand court and playgrounds;
Frederick Law Olmsted had designed
New York's Central Park.

67

Listed on the National Register of Historic Places, Branch Brook Park had been swampland surrounded by tenements.

Newark, N. J.   The Sand Court and Play Grounds, Branch Brook Park

68

Postcards were a great way to show civic pride. Located on the banks of the Passaic River, Montclair was once part of Newark and was referred to as Cranetown after *Red Badge of Courage* author Stephen Crane's ancestors, who lived there.

Greetings from MONTCLAIR N.J.

NEWARK AIRPORT. NEWARK. N. J. (SHOWING NEW ADMINISTRATION BUILDING)   14

Who'll bring home
the bacon
if Dad's not here?

Protect your family with Prudential life insurance
See your **Prudential Agent**

THE PRUDENTIAL INSURANCE COMPANY OF AMERICA • See "You Are There" Sundays CBS-TV • Hear Jack Berch Mon.-Fri. ABC radio

69

In 1934 WPA workers began building the art deco administration building.
Its cutting-edge style included construction of the control tower in the
building's middle. It opened May 16, 1935. The tower featured prominently
in a film that premiered the same year, *Ceiling Zero*, with James Cagney.

70

In 1873 Prudential got its start in a bank
basement as the Widows and Orphans
Friendly Society, selling "industrial" insurance
on "healthy lives" for ten dollars.

71

In the 1970s La Vogue Wig and Style Center
was located at 184 Clinton Avenue.
This postcard advertised
"Interlacing and Interweaving"
and "Wigs to the Trade Wholesale."

72

The new Pennsylvania Station opened for business on Raymond Plaza
on March 24, 1936. The art deco building, designed by McKim,
Mead and White, was a $42 million civic construction project
financed by Newark and the Pennsylvania Railroad Company.
Although mainly of Indiana limestone, the building's archways and base
were made from rubbed pink granite and its doors
of a new synthetic material called Formica.

Birthplace of Ex-President Cleveland, Caldwell, N. J. Hurry up and be Ex-President: so we may have this photo of your home. Grandma

CRYSTAL LAKE AMUSEMENT PARK (Playground of the Orange Mts.)

Eagle Rock Ave., West Orange, N. J.

73

The only U.S. president to be elected to nonconsecutive terms was born here at No. 1 Bloomfield Avenue on March 18, 1837. The son of a poor Presbyterian minister, Grover Cleveland was dubbed the bachelor president until he married Frances Folsom. He was both the twenty-second and twenty-fourth president. On display in Cleveland's birthplace museum is a gown worn by his daughter, Ruth, for whom the Baby Ruth candy bar was named.

74

Two miles from Newark, the Oranges developed as a recreation area for day-trippers going to the amusement park, outdoor enthusiasts to the horse-and-buggy trails and picnic groves in the Watchung Mountains, and eventually well-to-do commuters.

75

Rain didn't deter the good people of the Oranges, some three and four deep under their black umbrellas, from celebrating the Orange centennial on June 14, 1907. Seen here is the Seabury-Johnson float.

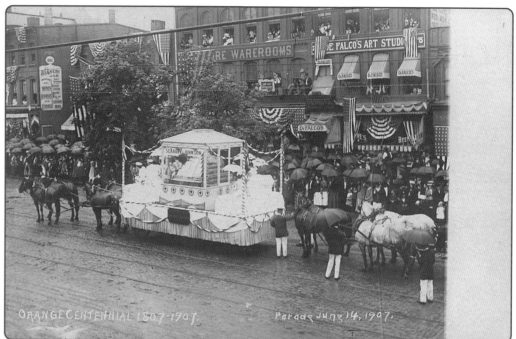

76

Opened in 1958, the South Mountain Arena in West Orange is used by two-time Stanley Cup–winners the New Jersey Devils as their practice rink.

Office of Thos. A. Edison, West Orange, N.J.   2425

Maplewood, N. J.   Rahway River

77

The Bill Gates–Steven Spielberg of his generation, Thomas Alva Edison stands in the doorway to his laboratories and factory on Lakeside Avenue in West Orange with some of his employees, whom he affectionately referred to as "muckers." The prolific Edison obtained patents for inventions that were the basis for the electric, telephone, recording, and movie industries. No scientific subject was too far afield to not try to make a go of it, whether it was rubber tires from the goldenrod plant or Portland cement as a fireproof building material. Edison set up shop in the Buttermilk Valley of the Watchung Range in 1887.

78

Immediately south of South Orange and four miles west of Newark's business center lies the suburban community of Maplewood.

B. Altman & Co., Short Hills
Morris Turnpike at River Road
Short Hills, N.J. Telephone Drexel 9-3000

PAPER MILL
PLAYHOUSE

MAIN ENTRANCE
PAPER MILL PLAYHOUSE   BROOKSIDE DRIVE
MILLBURN, N. J.

79

Responding to the entreaties of women who loved
to shop—transplanted New Yorkers lost in suburban
New Jersey—B. Altman & Company opened its first
suburban store here in 1957. It was the first anchor store
around which would develop The Mall at Short Hills.
By 1961 the open-air shopping arcade boasted
Bonwit Teller, FAO Schwartz, and Brentano's,
along with several dozen local retailers.

80

The first Actor's Equity house in New Jersey took hold in
the old Diamond Mill Paper Company millhouse in 1934.
The Kingdom of God, by Spanish playwright Gregorio
Martínez Sierra, opened the theater on November 14,
1938. Antoinette Scudder, an artist, poet, and playwright,
and Frank Carrington, an actor and theater director, were
the theater's driving forces. Regarded as a proving ground
for aspiring actors, the Paper Mill's stage has been graced
by the Gish sisters, Jason Robards, and Chita Rivera.

81
From 1862 to 1938 Joseph Castles
sold sweets and cigars. In 1890
he started offering ice cream
based on a recipe for frozen cream.

82

An early view of intermodal transportation on the Elizabeth waterfront on Newark Bay. Then, as now, cargo was exchanged between ships and trains.

83

Boxwood Hall, East Jersey Street, Elizabeth, owes its survival into the twenty-first century to its stint as an "old ladies' home" from 1870 to the mid-1930s. Washington visited here in 1789; the martyred Rev. James Caldwell was eulogized here; and Elias Boudinot, president of the Continental Congress, lived here. In the 1930s schoolchildren raised six thousand dollars to save the building from being demolished, and WPA workers restored Boxwood Hall to its original two-and-a-half story Georgian-style appearance. Today it is a state museum.

COMPANY No. 3, ELIZABETH, N. J. FIRE DEPARTMENT

ELIZABETH NOVELTY CO.

84

Washington Engine Company No. 3 was a paid fire company on Center Street at the time this picture was taken circa 1906. Built in the 1860s, the building was used as a warehouse by the city until it was torn down ten years ago.

11:—NEW JOURNAL BUILDING, ELIZABETH, N. J.

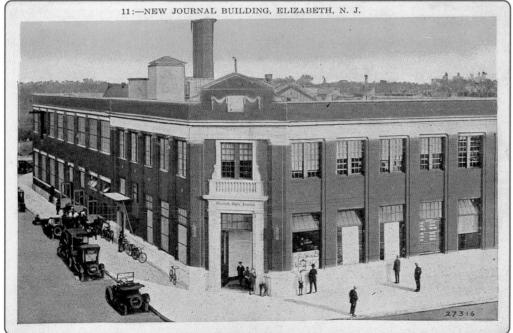

27316

85

The second oldest newspaper in the country after the *Hartford Courant* in Connecticut, the *Elizabeth Daily Journal* was started in 1779 by Chatham printer Shepard Kollock. It ceased its operations in 1992. The location shown here was at North Broad and Chestnut Streets.

86

The African Methodist Episcopal (A.M.E.) church movement started in the early nineteenth century in Philadelphia. It came to Elizabeth in 1830. In 1860 the Greater Mount Teman A.M.E. Church was established. In 1965 the congregation, under the leadership of Rev. L. Marshall Watts, built a new church on Madison Avenue uptown in the shopping district.

87

"Give 'em Watts, boys, give 'em Watts!" Presbyterian pastor Rev. James Caldwell is said to have cried. During the American Revolution Caldwell stuffed the soldiers' muskets with pages from the Watts hymnal after they ran short of gun wadding on June 23, 1780. Caldwell's wife, Hannah, had been killed two weeks previous in Union. Caldwell's act of heroism influenced Bret Harte to write the poem "Caldwell at Springfield." In 1781 Caldwell was shot through the heart at Elizabethtown Point by a Continental Army sentry who had been bribed.

THE STORY OF REVEREND CALDWELL

← Caldwell's Presbyterian Church, Springfield, N. J.

The Historic Caldwell Parsonage, Union, N. J.

BALTURSOL GOLF CLUB, NEAR SUMMIT, N. J.

88

Host to many a championship golf tournament, Baltusrol was established in 1895 on five hundred acres in Springfield Township owned by Louis Keller, publisher of the *New York Social Register*. The private golf club's name pays homage to the colonial farmer who owned the property before he was murdered. The present clubhouse was built after a fire in 1909 wiped out the original. Baltusrol's two eighteen-hole courses were designed by A. W. Tillinghast, who was known for incorporating natural landscaping into his courses.

Union, New Jersey

89

Part of the main shopping thoroughfare of Bergenline Avenue in Union. Billboard advertising helped encourage you to buy. Haydu hot dogs were made in Neptune in the Shore Region. Union was originally known as Connecticut Farms because its first settlers came from Connecticut in 1749.

90

From September 11, 1932, to May 4, 1933, "Wheatenaville Sketches" about "the town you'd like to live in" aired on WNBC radio starring Raymond Knight as Billy Batchelor. The breakfast cereal company, now owned by American Home Food Products, was located in Rahway during the 1930s.

Wheatenaville, Rahway, New Jersey

91

Diagonally bisecting New Jersey from New York to Philadelphia, Route 1 passed by a lot of different scenery, including the forbidding prison architecture of the facility used as a boy's state reformatory. It was built on state-owned farm property in Rahway in 1901.

Dining Room, New Jersey State Reformatory, Rahway, N. J.

200.591.JV

YE OLDE HISTORICAL INN, SCOTCH PLAINS, N. J.

92

According to recent excavations in which oyster and clam shells were unearthed, the Lenapes found this a natural habitation area. In the eighteenth century coach travelers on the York Road between Elizabethtown and Lambertville rested here. Today it's diners seeking out the French-inspired American cuisine at what is now the Stage House Inn.

ESSO RESEARCH CENTER, LINDEN, N. J.

93

One of the country's more influential petroleum companies, the Standard Oil Company evolved into Esso Corporation (now Exxon). It has had a corporate and industrial presence in New Jersey throughout most of the twentieth century, beginning in Newark before moving its corporate headquarters to Linden and then to Flemington to take advantage of favorable tax breaks.

94

Boynton Beach in Woodbridge Township's Sewaren section was a vacation destination on the sandy banks of Arthur Kill with a hotel, picnic grounds, shooting gallery, dance pavilion, roller coaster, and a daily steamboat from New York that operated in the summers from 1880 to 1900.

CANDY PAVILION

95

Established in 1865 as a canoe and rowing club, the Raritan Yacht Club is one of the oldest boat clubs in the country. It occupies the former home of the Cooper family, who have long been engaged in the oyster business on Raritan Bay. The club is the training site for the Princeton University sailing team.

Smith Street, showing Ferry, Perth Amboy, N. J.

96

The yellow slip from which little red ferries once shuttled day-trippers back and forth across Arthur Kill from Staten Island. The restored slip is now the northern way station on the New Jersey Coastal Heritage Trail.

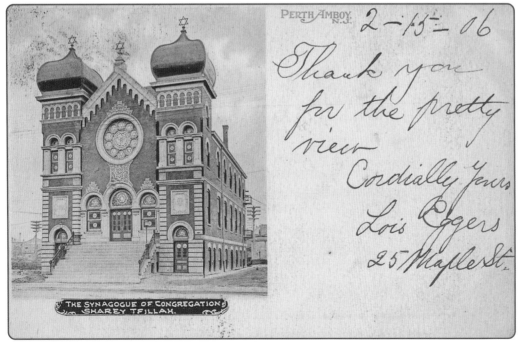

PERTH AMBOY, N.J.

2-15-06

Thank you for the pretty view

Cordially Yours

Lois Eggers

25 Maple St.

THE SYNAGOGUE OF CONGREGATION SHAREY TFILLAH.

97

This was the oldest synagogue in Middlesex County until a fire from the Good Guys discount store on Smith Street spread on the early afternoon of May 14, 1975, and destroyed the house of worship built in 1903 on Madison Avenue. The synagogue was unusual in that it also contained a mikvah, or ceremonial bathhouse for Orthodox married women. The Congregation Shaarey Tefiloh (Hebrew for "Gates of Prayer") began in 1890. The Young Men's Hebrew Association is there today.

HENRY FORD AND THOMAS A. EDISON

98

The Edison Tower was built in 1937 on the site
of the inventor's laboratory and dedicated
the following year. Here Thomas Edison invented
the first successful incandescent lamp
and the phonograph. To commemorate these
inventions, a glass replica of the original lamp
is mounted on the tower. At one time,
phonograph records of carillons and other
music were broadcast from the tower and
could be heard over a two-mile radius.

99

Detroit motor mogul Henry Ford idolized Thomas Edison so much
that he removed the inventor's Menlo Park laboratory
and reconstructed it at his museum in Dearborn, Michigan.

THE WALKER-GORDON "ROTOLACTOR," PLAINSBORO, N. J.

100

The Rotolactor—the cow merry-go-round exclusive to the Walker-Gordon Farm—was located on Route 1 in Plainsboro. Once billed as the world's largest certified milk farm, with twenty-eight hundred cows on twenty-four hundred acres, the farm produced twenty-six thousand quarts of milk daily. It took only eighteen minutes for the cows to be showered, dried, and milked. The milk was never exposed to human hands or outside air. It reached customers within one day of milking.

THIS IS THE KIND WE GROW IN NEW BRUNSWICK, N.J,

101

This novelty postcard expresses a sentiment well known in the Garden State. In 1759 Swedish botanist Peter Kalm, traveling through the Raritan River Valley, remarked that the corn was "usually eight feet high, more or less [and] every countryman had an orchard full of peach trees which were covered with such quantities of fruit that we could scarcely walk in the orchard without treading upon the peaches that had fallen off."

102

Robert Wood Johnson and his brothers built a factory at one end of George Street near the Raritan River in New Brunswick to make a new, ready-made, sterile surgical dressing that was wrapped and sealed in individual packages and suitable for instant use without the risk of contamination. The company's scientific director was Fred B. Kilmer, father of the poet Joyce Kilmer.

Johnson & Johnson's Factory, New Brunswick, N. J.

1074

103

This bird's-eye view shows where the Delaware and Raritan Canal and Raritan River came together.

NB-15—Bird's-Eye View of New Brunswick, N. J., Showing Raritan River and Municipal Dock

9A-H555

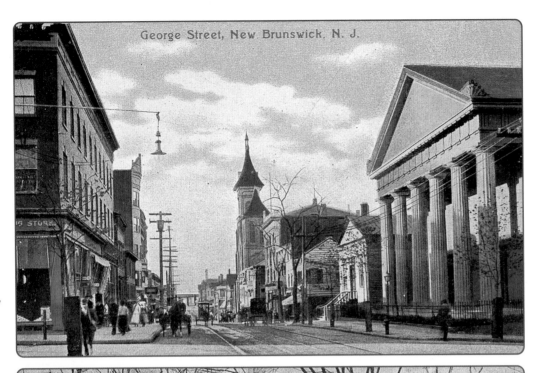

George Street, New Brunswick, N. J.

104

New Brunswick's main thoroughfare as seen in the late nineteenth century.

Gateway to Rutgers College, NEW BRUNSWICK, N. J.

105

The historic gates to Rutgers University, through which can be seen Kirkpatrick Chapel. Rutgers University was founded in 1766 as Queens College for the purpose of educating ministers for the Dutch Reformed Church. Rutgers College became a state institution in 1864. Before the American Revolution, New Jersey was the only colony with two colleges; the other was Princeton.

MAIN-GATE ENTRANCE   CAMP KILMER, N.J.

106

Poet Joyce Kilmer was born in New Brunswick on December 6, 1886,
and died in France during World War I on July 30, 1918.
The Rutgers College graduate who taught Latin for one year
in Morristown high school went on to become a reporter for
the *New York Times* before enlisting. The thirty-two-year old wrote
a lot of Victorian poetry infused with religious and nature imagery,
none more famous than "Trees." Some of the titles to his other poems
are "Pennies," "Alarm Clocks," and "Stars." This World War II military camp
was named in his honor. Part of the property remains in military use as an
army reserve training facility, and part of it is the Piscataway campus
of Rutgers University, including the offices of the Rutgers University Press.

The Rustic Life

SKYLANDS REGION

The impulse to get closer to nature didn't first happen in the 1960s. It really happened nearly one hundred years earlier when people went to fish in the river valleys that ripple off the Appalachian Trail in New Jersey's northwest corner and when they went to hunt in the woods off remote streams or ride with the hounds through the piedmont's more manicured glens. It happened when they built cabins they returned to with their friends or comfortable cottages large enough to hold three generations and guests for the summer season. It happened when they took to whittling wood or more likely buying paperweights, cups, and fancy picture holders made from the native maple, chestnut, elm, sassafras, and birch. It happened on Lake Hopatcong's forty-five miles of crenellated shoreline in 1880 as timbered hotels and homes vied with roomy canvas tents for a piece of the nine-mile-long water view. And again on the more modestly sized Budd Lake. And again on Swartswood. And later on Lake Mohawk, Green Pond, and Cranberry Lake.

Both the Morris and Delaware and Raritan Canals tried the travel trade, catering to those looking for a calm water excursion through a rural setting. Meanwhile, George Washington's headquarters and Tempe Wick's house in Morristown sparked tourist curiosity when the federal government made them part of America's first National Historical Park in 1933. Original Minisink Indian trails south and east from the Delaware River that became colonial market roads turned into touring roads. Instead of leading to Camden, the Amboys, and Newark, they led away from those cities' paved streets and back to the land. Along those routes tobacco heiress Doris Duke opened her family's gardens to the public. The religious, the not-so-religious, and the state opened sanitariums. Farmers began converting their roadside properties into auto camps, grill rooms, fast-food eateries, and family-friendly amusement parks.

New Jersey's mountain and lakes region not only attracted city photographers like William Broadwell and A. J. Bloom but also the English-born, Pennsylvania-reared William J. Harris and Hackettstown's own George Scheller, who is still at work today producing chrome postcards. The region also attracted at least one woman photographer, Mary Sunderlin of Flemington. Sometime around 1900 William J. Harris set up his photo shop on Lake Hopatcong. Literally. He worked on a buoyant rig he referred to as his photo float. Harris took it around most of the lake's 2,443 acres—the state's largest inland lake—until a mishap led him to set up at the Breslin Hotel for a while. Later he moved next door to Lee's Pavilion on Nolan's Point. Not a shy man by any means, he had painted on one wall: "HARRIS the POST CARD MAN." Robert R. Goller, writing in volume twenty-eight of "El Escribano," the *St. Augustine Journal of History* (1991), described the mustached photographer as tall and lanky with an authoritative voice, a flair for novelty and promotion, an ever-present cigar, and a little dog named Hypo that he often photographed. He was young. He was a widower. And he had time to develop a career.

Having attended the 1893 World's Columbian Exposition in Chicago, Harris started advertising his stock of souvenir private mailing cards in 1902. The response was overwhelming and kept Harris and his staff busy around the clock making photo postcards of hotels and his signature sunset and clouds views he had taken along the lake.

By 1904, with the demand for postcards greater than ever, Harris launched a line of comic novelty cards beginning with "It Floats." The view showed a man dressed in a woman's bathing costume that had been pumped full of air. Looking like an obese woman, he stood with his back to the camera, holding a parasol. Harris's inscription was simply, "It Floats." Before long, pirated versions of Harris's postcard began turning up in other waterfront resorts such as Asbury Park and Atlantic City. Harris also launched a series of photo cards that bore various inscriptions from sentimental charm to humor over the rites of courtship and marriage.

By this point, too, postcard publishing companies were issuing machine-printed cards—black-and-white, hand-colored, and machine-colored—available everywhere for a penny a piece or less. During the summer of 1909 Harris produced more than two hundred thousand postcards, an exhausting amount. By 1910 he had four hundred different views of Lake Hopatcong. Two years later he finally turned to the Curt Teich Company of Chicago to mass produce his cards in color.

Eventually remarried and with children, Harris divided his time between Lake Hopatcong and St. Augustine, Florida, another popular tourist destination where he became curator of the historical society. He left behind some of the most highly collectible photo cards of New Jersey.

Over time, the nineteenth century's back-to-the-land movement made such a nostalgic impression that, years later, nearly all of those rustic addresses are now year-round residences.

Sussex, Hunterdon, Somerset, Warren, and Morris Counties make up the Skylands Region.

World War Memorial Monument, 220 Feet High 43

High Point Park, near Port Jervis, N. Y.

HIGH POINT PARK, N J.

The Rustic Life

67

107

The base of this 220-foot-tall monument stands on the highest point in New Jersey, 1,803 feet above sea level. Dedicated in 1930, the windows of the stone tower offer vistas overlooking New Jersey's Kittatinny Mountains, Pennsylvania's Poconos, and New York's Catskills, plus the Delaware and Neversink Rivers. On a clear day you can see the Delaware Water Gap eighty miles to the south and portions of the Appalachian Trail, which runs through the park.

108

High Point Inn was put up in 1888 and taken down in 1996. It overlooked Lake Marcia, the state's highest freshwater lake at sixteen hundred feet above sea level. It was named for the French-Canadian girlfriend of the surveyor hired by Colonel and Mrs. Anthony Kuser of Bernardsville, who donated ten thousand acres along the Kittatinny Mountains to the state in 1923. At one time the park even had reindeer paddocks and a bear pit at the southern tip of Lake Marcia.

Main St., Sussex, N. J.

109

By the middle of the twentieth century, New Jersey had a $65-million-a-year dairy industry. Sussex County was known for its registered Guernseys, while the village of Sussex was the largest milk-receiving station in the state, meriting a Lackawanna Railroad stop just for milk cars.

110

The rabbit hutch that went awry: Playboy Great Gorge had seven hundred rooms, a twenty-seven-hole championship golf course, indoor and outdoor tennis courts, five restaurants, a cabaret venue, a discothèque, and enough convention space for up to four thousand people—all in the tiny village of McAfee within the vast township of Vernon. When Playboy Enterprises stumbled in the 1980s, so did this high-heeled alpine resort. In the last years of the twentieth century the property's new name became the Legends Resort and Country Club.

111

The YMCA headquarters in Newark operated a statewide camp for boys on Lake Wawayanda from 1885 to 1919, when the property was bought by the American Zinc Company. The YMCA then moved to Andover, taking the lake's Indian name with it (it means water on the mountain). In 1954 the YMCA relocated the camp to New York State. In the aftermath of World War I, YMCA boys received military-type training as part of the YMCA's emphasis on duty to God and country.

RIFLE RANGE, CAMP WAWAYANDA, N. J. STATE Y.M.C.A. CAMP FOR BOYS, ANDOVER, N. J.

112

John P. Muller built the most elaborate vacation home on the River Styx and named it for his son. Seen here circa 1905, the seventeenth-century-inspired castle hotel was in its infancy with only one story and twenty rooms, including a ballroom, bowling alleys, and a billiards parlor. The nightly rate was twelve dollars. To the right was the family's original boathouse when the property was still called Camp Edward. A fire in 1931 destroyed the hotel.

CASTLE EDWARD, LAKE HOPATCONG, N. J.

Lake Hopatcong, N. J.   River Styx Bridge

ALAMAC HOTEL, MT. ARLINGTON, N. J., ON LAKE HOPATCONG.

COPYRIGHT 1914, W. J. HARRIS

113 & 114

The northern cousin to the Jersey Devil lived here, according to local lore: it had a horse's head,
an elephant's body, and a ten-foot spread of antlers. Undeterred, vacationers came anyway.
Some stayed at the Breslin Hotel, known in 1918 as the Alamac, where Abbott and Costello
stayed and played, as did Milton Berle and his mother. It burned in 1948.

Unique Gingerbread Castle,
Designed by Joseph Urban, Hamburg, N. J.

115 & 116

Designed by Joseph Urban, Flo Ziegfeld's and the Metropolitan Opera's scene designer,
the Gingerbread Castle was inspired by the operetta *Hansel and Gretel*. Commissioned by businessperson
F. W. Bennet, who wanted to re-create the land of fairy tales, the castle had Humpty Dumpty sitting on a wall,
Prince Charming astride his prancing charger, a black cat guarding the turret, and a witch's trophy room
in the dungeon. Gingerbread cookies and peppermint sticks studded the walls. The castle was finished in 1930
at a cost of $250,000. Located on Route 23, it is open in the summer and on Halloween.

Swartswood, N. J.

117 & 118
A look back at what attracted
vacationers . . .

Green Pond, N. J.

Manitou Island, Lake Mohawk, near Newton, N. J.

119 & 120
. . . in the first place.

THE PAVILLION, CRANBERRY LAKE, N. J.

121
The Delaware Water Gap, where Route 80, Worthington State Forest, and Pennsylvania connect at the Delaware River.

MYERS FERRY
DELAWARE, N.J.

122
There was more than one way to get to Pennsylvania. A rider with a horse and carriage used the flat-bottomed ferryboat from Delaware in Knowlton Township.

123

The Land of Make Believe in Hope: what names could go better together? In 1954 a dairy farm was converted into the summer-only amusement park.

124

In 1944 John Kovalsky left the coal mines in Dover to open up a stand on Route 46 in Buttzville, which his daughter still manages. With the Pequest River running through it on its way to the Delaware, Buttzville is a rustic, trout-fishing paradise.

JUNCTION OF THE LEHIGH AND DELAWARE RIVERS.

SHOWING EASTON ON THE LEFT AND FAIR VIEW HEIGHTS, PHILLIPSBURG, N. J., ON THE RIGHT.

125

At Phillipsburg, the Delaware River is joined by the Lehigh out of the Pennsylvania watershed. The Delaware's most northern industrial city, Phillipsburg was linked to Newark first by the Morris Canal and then by the Pennsylvania Railroad.

View on Morris Canal, Hackettstown, N. J.

126

Besides hauling Pennsylvania coal, canal boats were also used as excursion vehicles at various points along the canal route. The Morris Canal comprised eleven inclined planes and seven lift locks—no small engineering feat. Lake Hopatcong was dammed to provide a constant water supply to the canal. The canal's chief designer, George Macculloch of Morristown, was interested in seeing Pennsylvania coal get to the iron foundries in Morris County.

127

Hospitality came to Helm's Mills when, as the local legend has it, land baron Sam Hackett hosted an open bar to christen the new hotel in town and thus triggered a name change to Hackettstown in 1768. This otherwise quiet little mountain town is bisected by the industrial roar of Route 46.

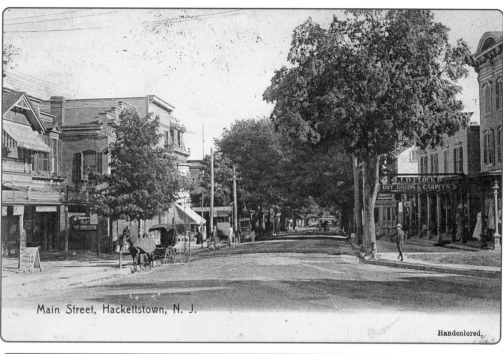

Main Street, Hackettstown, N. J.

Handcolored.

128

Tumbling out of Bowling Green Mountain north of Lake Hopatcong, the Musconetcong River flows forty-four miles southwest before emptying into the Delaware, creating a fertile limestone river valley between Allamuchy and Pohatcong Mountains to the north and Schooley's and Musconetcong Mountains to the south. It is another popular fishing mecca.

MUSCONETCONG TROUT STREAM, HACKETTSTOWN, N. J.

1A2867

Girls' Parlor, C. C. I., Hackettstown, N. J.

Dorset Breeding-Ewes, Tranquility Farms, Allamuchy, N. J.

129
Hackettstown is home to Centenary College,
founded in 1867 as a finishing school
for privileged young women. In 1976
it began offering four-year degrees,
and in 1988 men were admitted.

130
Allamuchy Mountain, named after the Indian word for "place of cocoons,"
is still the backdrop for Tranquility Farms, although today
the agribusiness is a fresh produce and dairy concern.

Budd's Beach, Budd Lake, N. J.   6

131 & 132

There are at least eighteen postcards produced in this linen series on Budd Lake, New Jersey's resort amusement equivalent to Lake George, New York, where cottages were once hung with such 1920s' idyllic names as the Dew Drop Inn and the Aw-Kum-On Inn. The town hall has since been relocated.

Municipal Building and Beach, Budd Lake, N. J.   1

MUNICIPAL BUILDING

133
Wild West City in Netcong along Lake Musconetcong still draws crowds more than forty years after the Stabile family opened its gates to day-trippers. Bob Little Hawk Martin carries on the tradition of dance presentations started by his uncle, Art Big Mountain, who was part Mohawk Indian. New Jersey comedian Uncle Floyd got his showbiz start singing honky-tonk tunes in Wild West City's saloon.

St. Francis Health Resort

Denville, New Jersey

134
Denville was a Lackawanna Railroad junction anchored at one end by Indian Lake. Not far away flowed the Rockaway River. The water provided the necessary element for the creation of a health resort in 1895 run by the Sisters of the Sorrowful Mother of the Third Order of St. Francis, which is still in operation.

135

The most curious Revolutionary War site to be saved from the wrecking ball has to be the 1750 Morristown family home of twenty-one-year-old Tempe Wick, whose father was a colonial colonel. According to popular legend, she saved her beloved white stallion from being taken into His Majesty's royal service by hiding the four-legged beast in her family's modest frame home for three days. The building is located in the Jockey Hollow section of the Morristown National Historical Park.

THE HOME OF TEMPE WICK OF REVOLUTIONARY FAME, MORRISTOWN, N. J. 6

136

George Washington really did sleep here in the notoriously cold winter of 1779–80. So did Martha, thanks to the hospitality of Theodosia Ford, a widow who offered her Georgian mansion for use as the military headquarters for the Continental Army. This mansion ranks next to Mount Vernon in its collection of Washington artifacts.

G 2092 Washington's Headquarters, Morristown, N. J.

Home of the Morse Telegraph,
Morristown, N. J.

137
Just north of the Whippany River, painter, inventor, and tireless self-promoter Samuel F. B. Morse and his shyer, quieter partner Alfred Vail wrapped a barn on the Vail property with three miles of magnetic wire one January day in 1838. With Vail scribbling down the letters as he received what would come to be called Morse code, Morse sent the message: "A patient waiter is no loser."

MUNICIPAL BUILDING SHOWING THE POOL AND THE WORLD WAR MEMORIAL. SOUTH STREET, MORRISTOWN, N. J.

(TAKEN FROM THE STEEPLE OF THE ST. PETER'S CHURCH)

138
Alfred Vail's cousin, Theodore, became the first president of the American Telephone and Telegraph Company and in 1916, as one of the signs of his wealth, built a Renaissance palazzo across from St. Peter's Episcopal Church. He died before he could move in. His niece sold the mansion to Morristown for $51,183, and it was used as municipal offices until recently, when it was sold to a real estate developer with plans to turn it into a hotel and restaurant.

THE HEADQUARTERS OF THE SEEING EYE, INC.
near Morristown, N. J.

Madison, N. J. Brook Lake Chime Tower, Dr. Ward's Park

139
A woman with a vision for helping those who could not see
and a man who was blind established the Seeing Eye Institute in Whippany.
Dorothy Harrison Eustis saw the work being done in Europe to help
World War I soldiers who had been blinded regain their independence with
the help of specially trained dogs and brought the idea back to the States.
The institute was the first of its kind in America.
It moved to Morristown in 1965.

140
Madison's Dr. Leslie Ward, a Prudential
Life Insurance vice president, built an estate in
nearby Florham Park and opened its seven miles
of road to the public. He also built a wooden
clock tower from whose spire the Belgian carillon
bells could be heard on the half hour. The tower
burned to the ground in 1967. There are
condominiums on the site today.

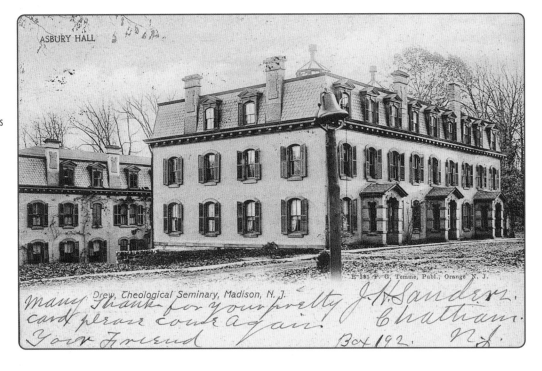

ASBURY HALL

Drew, Theological Seminary, Madison, N. J.

E-895 F. G. Temme, Publ., Orange N. J.

Many thanks for your pretty card please come again. Your Friend

J. H. Sanders. Chatham. Box 192. N. J.

141
William Gibbons built an estate in the late 1830s that became Drew Theological Seminary in 1866. The Methodist institute became a liberal arts college in 1928. Asbury Hall, named for Francis Asbury, who brought Methodism to the colonies, was the former Gibbons stable, cleaned and converted into a dormitory still in use.

142 & 143

What stays and what's lost to progress. Madison began as a way station between Elizabethtown and Hackettstown, called Bottle Hill because the tavern owner was said to have hung an empty bottle from a nearby tree limb. There is a bank on its site today. In Whitehouse, Mike and Ted Ryman started the Ryland Inn, whose country charm and award-winning cuisine endures despite encroaching commercial development on Route 28.

F. C. WILLIAMS PRODUCE MARKET—Wholesale and Retail—North Branch, N. J.
Largest on Route 28 From New York to Easton

144 & 145

Before and after: this was one roadside farm stand that took advantage of the state's upgrade of the original New Jersey Turnpike to Easton, Pennsylvania, and what Garden State produce looked like in the hands of a creative chef at the once famous Far Hills Inn. The eatery on Route 31 north of Somerville has since burned down. Williams's market is now known as the North Branch General Store. This 1830s village is situated on the north branch of the Raritan River.

146

The rival canal to the Morris Canal, the Delaware and Raritan Canal winds its way through Bound Brook, past one of the many paint and chemical factories once located there.

147

The French-born Pathé brothers worked with the Du Pont chemical company to make film for Hollywood in 1923. Long before there were movie trailers, Pathé newsreel footage was shown before feature films. By the 1930s the independent company was on its way out.

ENSEMBLE BROADCAST—WAWZ STUDIO
Alma White College (Pillar of Fire), Zarephath, N. J.

148
The severe fire that nearly wiped out
this Revolutionary War–era town in 1881
led to the establishment of four fire companies,
which Bound Brook was proud to promote
in this civic postcard.

149
South of Bound Brook, on an island between the Raritan and the canal,
is Zarephath. The Pillar of Fire religious sect was formed there in 1901
by Alma White, a Methodist minister's wife, and was named
after the light in Exodus that led the Israelites through the wilderness.
The name Zarephath came from the town in 1 Kings where the widow
fed the prophet Elijah. At the sect's height, there were forty-three
Pillar of Fire temples from London to San Francisco.

150

A pretty thorough use of postcard
advertising.

151

152

Because of the delicate piece of fabric cut for
her jacket and glued to the card, this is known
as a "silk" to collectors. In this series of postcards
designed to represent the states, the woman
representing New Jersey is dressed in an 1890s
riding outfit. Coincidentally, a 1916 estate in
Peapack was converted into the U.S. Equestrian
Team Olympic Training Center, which is open
to the public for equine sporting events.

From its French parterre garden to its tropical jungle under glass,
Duke Gardens features eleven geographically and culturally
distinct environments.

153 & 154

Originally part of the Duke tobacco family estate, this botanical site was opened to the public in 1964.

Wallace House, SOMERVILLE, N. J.

155

George and Martha Washington also slept here in the country home of Philadelphia merchant John Wallace, who later retired here after the Revolution. Today it is a state historic site.

156

Green Sergeant's Bridge, the state's last nineteenth-century covered bridge, is located just outside the Sergeantsville section of Delaware Township on the Rosemont-Sergeantsville Road. It was built about 1872 over the Wickecheoke Creek using stone abutments from a previous bridge put up in 1860.

157

"Jersey Pork" was an agricultural tradition and one of the few to remain in the state long after beef cattle and sheep moved west. Frank Bird of Stanton Mill in Readington Township used these porkers to advertise his feed business: "The best and safest feeds on earth for brood sows, young pigs, chickens, and turkeys. High protein feed for dairy cows. Concentrated feed for laying hens."

158

No traffic circle in New Jersey is complete without a diner catering to traveling motorists and locals alike. This was the original Circle Diner in Flemington before it burned.

UNION HOTEL, FLEMINGTON, N. J.

159

Originally built in 1718 and rebuilt in 1862 after a fire, the Union Hotel still stands across the street from the courthouse, and the public can still eat in its dining room, though the hotel is closed to overnight guests.

Flemington Athletic Field, 1915.

160

Playing America's national pastime.

161

Mary Sunderlin photographed these women who dressed in Japanese kimonos to sell ice cream on the midway for Crazy Days on the Flemington Fairgrounds in 1908.

162

Originally known as Coryell's Ferry, the town was eventually named for John Lambert, who opened a post office in this riverbank community in 1812.

Union Street Looking South, LAMBERTVILLE, N. J.

Shad Fishing,   Lambertville, N. J.

163

Every year in the early spring,
Lambertville commemorates the
annual shad run up the Delaware
with a festival. Shad were once so
plentiful that people would dip
bushel baskets in the shad run
and pull up a full load.

164

St. John Terrell's Music Circus
on top of Music Mountain in
Lambertville laid claim to being
the country's first, and original,
tent theater. The property is
currently slated for a housing
development in which the streets
will be named after well-known
musicals.

Down the River, over Creeks, in the Pines

DELAWARE RIVER REGION

Just as the steamboat- and locomotive-designing Stevens family of Hoboken helped to change how we could travel in America, the Roeblings of Trenton helped to change where we could. From his wire-cable mills, scion John A. Roebling began by building the first railroad suspension bridge across Niagara Falls. Next he built a one over the Ohio River in Cincinnati. Then in 1867 he designed the Brooklyn Bridge. In the next century, his descendents built the George Washington Bridge connecting New Jersey to New York and later the Golden Gate Bridge in San Francisco.

Factories along the banks of the Delaware River, Assunpink Creek, and the Delaware and Raritan Canal not only filled the nation's growing transportation needs but its growing desire for consumer goods as well. The state capital's industries made the anvils to forge the country's iron. They also made rubber, wall plaster, cars, farm tools, mattresses, watches, bricks, linoleum, cigars, and the custom porcelain tub for the 350-pound president, William

Howard Taft. The porcelain didn't stop there either. Walter Lenox launched a line of dinnerware baked from the abundant clay in the local soil.

By 1911 the Trenton Chamber of Commerce was so proud of the seemingly limitless line of products coming out of the city's factories that it sponsored a slogan contest. A total of 1,476 entries were submitted. The winning words came from S. Roy Heath, heir to a lumber company and future senator. Heath had a talent for rhyme and promotion. For the family company he came up with: "If it's in the woods, Heath can furnish the goods." For the chamber's contest, Heath entered, "The World Takes—Trenton Makes." His slogan won. Six years later the catchy phrase was rearranged to "Trenton Makes—The World Takes" and installed in large letters on the cast-iron bridge across the Delaware linking the city to Morrisville, Pennsylvania.

Camden was no less industrious at producing products Americans could use for leisure. In 1894 a customer came into Eldridge R. Johnson's general repair shop with a crude talking machine. Johnson not only fixed it but, after some time studying it, changed the design, substituting a flat, circular, phonographic disk for the original cylinders. Voilà! The first Victor talking machine. Singers and musicians came to Camden from all over the world to be recorded. Fans wrote to the Victor Talking Machine Company for publicity photographs of their favorite performers. In 1927 the Radio Corporation of America bought the business that became known as RCA Victor.

Esterbrook made pens, Carter Paper Company made Viking toilet tissue, J. B. Van Sciver made furniture, and the New York Shipbuilding Company built cargo and military vessels. Joseph Campell made fruit preserves in a small factory on the southwest corner of Second and Market Streets. Then a chemist came along and figured out how to condense soups made from vegetables grown in the Garden State. Months after the vegetables had been harvested, Campbell's Soup was tasting good to consumers attracted to the time-saving novelty of buying soup in a can.

Much of the produce came from Salem County, a round shoulder of land at the mouth of the Delaware. The county seat, Salem, was the first permanent English-speaking settlement on the bay, and it was from here in 1803 that the peripatetic Zadock Street and his sons left New Jersey, making their way west to the new territories. As they went, they seeded a little bit of their hometown's spirit, founding towns in Ohio, Indiana, Iowa, and Oregon and naming them all Salem.

A huge coastal plain of wilderness filled with botanicals and hardwoods and teeming with such game as turkey, bear, raccoons, and birds backs this region's river cities. It attracted the soft-spoken Elizabeth White, who cultivated blueberries, and the hard-nosed entrepreneur Joseph Wharton, who wanted to export water from the aquifer under the pines to Philadelphia.

Both before and after the American Revolution, pine and cedar lumber moved out of the Pine Barrens to shipyards on the Delaware and to nearby towns. But as the timber industry shifted out of state, the roads used by loggers, as well as charcoal burners and bog iron smelters, were taken over by hunters, honeymooners, berry pickers, and canoeists. If you wanted to get away from all the civilization along both sides of the Delaware River, getting lost in the pinelands of the state's largest county, Burlington, could bring you all the way to saltwater, where the Mullica, Wading, and Bass Rivers empty into Great Bay on the Atlantic Ocean.

The bulk of New Jersey that is below the Trenton-Manasquan waistline is blessed with a climate temperate not only for agriculture but also for out-of-doors photography. Notable photographers who produced regional postcards were William J. Cooper of Medford, William Bradwell of Hancock's Bridge, and the Thorburns of Hightstown. The first Thorburn, known simply as R. Thorburn, arrived about 1879, stayed for a few years, and left. Edward B. Thorburn of New York arrived about ten years later. Both a photographer and a skilled engraver, the younger Thorburn specialized in photographing important buildings in and around the geographically pivotal mill-town-cum-railroad-hub, such as interior and exterior views of schools, churches, hotels, and railroad stations. Edward Thorburn did his engravings on steel, silver, and gold, and his photo-engravings for newspaper cuts were regarded as some of the best in the state. He also made picture postcards to order.

Mercer, Burlington, Gloucester, Camden, and Salem Counties make up the Delaware River Region.

Roebling's Wire Mills, Trenton, N.J.

165

Roebling not only made cables for suspension bridges but also antisubmarine netting, artillery chains, and other arms used in World War I. The last remaining factory building in the compound is today the restaurant and dance club Katmandu.

A View of some of the Potteries, Trenton, N.J.

63822

166

The manufacture of pottery began to thrive in Trenton in 1850 as English and Irish artisans came to teach the trade. By 1880 Trenton, which was built on clay, was nicknamed the Staffordshire of America and was home of the first American-made Belleek china. The first porcelain sanitary commodes also were made in Trenton.

167 & 168

The state fairgrounds in Hamilton is the site of Grounds for Sculpture, created by sculptor and Johnson & Johnson heir J. Seward Johnson Jr., and a French-inspired restaurant named Rat's after a beloved character in the beguiling children's tale *The Wind in the Willows*.

Down
the River,
over
Creeks,
in the Pines

101

State House from River, Trenton, N. J.   With best regards .C.   97-18

LEGIS LATIVE CHAMBER IN THE STATE CAPITOL.

TRENTON N J

169 & 170

New Jersey was among the first of the colonies to declare its independence from the British Crown and in 1784 was briefly under consideration to be the capital of the United States. Trenton was made the state capital in 1790. A mix of building styles, the statehouse's original core dates from 1792; its gilded cupola dates from 1889; and it has a French Renaissance facade. The legislative chamber has recently been restored.

171

Undeniably one of the more famous postcards to capture the river city's once proud business spirit.

172

Located on South Willow and Front Streets, this is the last remaining of five barracks that alternately housed Continental, Hessian, and British troops, the last during the French and Indian War of 1763. The barracks were built in 1758 of native fieldstone. Now a state museum, it is a popular destination as a field trip for elementary school children from all over the state.

NEW JERSEY STATE BARRACKS, BUILT IN 1758, TRENTON, N. J.

State Street Lock, Delaware and Raritan Canal, Trenton, N.J.

63800

173

With a charter in 1830 and construction completed by 1832, the ambitious forty-two-mile-long canal between Bordentown and New Brunswick was logging upward of 115 barges a day through the capital. Its chief cargo was coal from Pennsylvania.

McConkey Homestead, Washington's Crossing, N.J.
Geo. Washington stayed here all night the night before the battle of Trenton.

63831

174

Though the McConkey family lived in Pennsylvania, the ferry service they operated came ashore here at a tavern near Titusville. Restored, the building is part of Washington Crossing State Park, north of Trenton.

175
The paddle wheeler plied
the Delaware River between the
capital city and Camden, making
the excursion an ideal day trip.

Trenton, N. J. Steamer "Burlington".

Down
the River,
over
Creeks,
in the Pines

105

176
Miller and landowner John Hight
gave his name to this town,
a market hub for surrounding
farms, in 1721. The water falls
from Peddie Lake.

THE FALLS, HIGHTSTOWN, N. J.

Railroad Hotel, Erected 1783, Hightstown, N. J.

207.290. (JV)

177

In 1834 Hightstown became a station on the Camden & Amboy Railroad. Though the outside has been modified, this building is still standing.

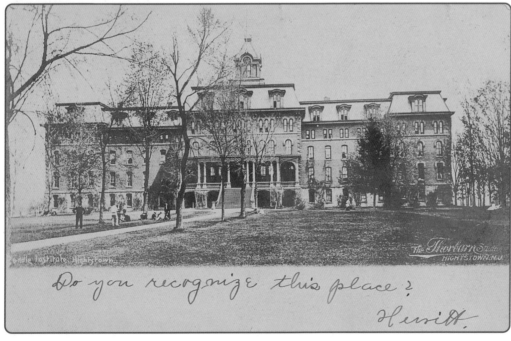

Peddie Institute, Hightstown.

The Thorburn Studio
HIGHTSTOWN, N.J.

Do you recognize this place?

Hewitt.

178

A promotional view of the 1864 Peddie Institute taken by the Thorburn Studio.

179

The tiger became Princeton University's mascot in the early 1880s.

Down
the River,
over
Creeks,
in the Pines

107

180

Princeton University moved to this sandstone building constructed in 1756, though the college had originally opened in Elizabeth in 1747. By 1911 bronze tigers flanked the entrance steps.

NASSAU INN, PRINCETON, N. J.

181

The Nassau Inn, a colonial stagecoach stop, at its original location on Nassau Street.

Blair Hall and Station, Princeton, N. J.

182

Blair Hall, named for elementary school dropout and railroad investor John I. Blair of Warren County, rises behind the "Dinky" station. The abbreviated rail line linking downtown Princeton to the major north-south rail route in Princeton Junction was built in 1865.

183

Diplomat, soldier, king of Naples, and king of Spain until his younger brother Napoleon was crushed at the Battle of Waterloo, Joseph Bonaparte spent most of his self-imposed exile in the early 1800s in Bordentown, not far from the Philadelphia–to–New York railroad route. Now restored, this gardener's house is all that remains of his estate on the Delaware bluffs.

The Old Bonaparte Park House, Bordentown, N. J.

184

Founder of the American Red Cross, Clara Barton started as a schoolteacher here in 1851, establishing one of the state's first free public schools for poor children. She resigned when the townspeople insisted that her work be supervised by a male principal.

SCHOOL HOUSE IN WHICH CLARA BARTON, LATE PRES. OF RED CROSS SOCIETY, ONCE TAUGHT, BORDENTOWN, N. J.

HANDCOLORED

RIVER BANK, BEVERLY, N.J.

Shore Club Houses, Delanco, N. J.

185, 186, 187, & 188
Scenes from the Delaware, heading
downstream: Beverly and Delanco
in Burlington County; Billingsport,
part of Greenwich Township in
Gloucester County; and Penn's
Grove in Salem County.

River front at Billingsport, New Jersey

Down
the River,
over
Creeks,
in the Pines

111

"Ulrica" at Pier, Penn's Grove, New Jersey

Public Library, Burlington, N. J. (Chartered by King George II, 1757.)

189

The oldest continuing library in New Jersey was chartered in Burlington in 1757 by King George II of England.

Home of J. Fenimore Cooper, Burlington, N.J. Built in 1689

190

Historic High Street in Burlington boasts the birthplaces of (left) *Last of the Mohicans* author James Fenimore Cooper (1789) and Captain James Lawrence (1781), naval hero most famous for the rallying cry, "Don't give up the ship," during the War of 1812.

191
Many a butcher and restaurant cook learned the trade by
feeding the thousands of enlisted men at this eighty-seven-hundred-acre
military base in New Hanover Township, seen here in this
World War I–era photo card.

Down
the River,
over
Creeks,
in the Pines

ﻟﯿﺒﯩﺮ

113

192
"Life At Camp Dix. Two is a company,
three is a crowd, and four is a mob.
You can't get away from those spooner spoofers.
They even hide in the hollow of a tree to spoil
a delightful evening." Military censors read the
backs of postcards to make sure no sensitive
information was revealed.

193

In Medford Lakes it was a different kind of camp life at the Robert Simpson Hotel twenty miles from Philadelphia. Seen here is the lobby of the main cabin for the compound known as Log Cabin Lodge. It billed itself as a "honeymoon haven." Known more recently as Settlers Inn, the lodge was destroyed by fire on January 10, 1998.

THE CANOE CLUB   BROWN'S MILLS IN THE PINES, N. J.

194

Brown's Mills in the Pines, located near the headwaters of Rancocas Creek, was another rustic hideaway in the Pine Barrens. It began as a health resort for people with tuberculosis.

195

This postcard advertises a
Maple Shade motel: "Most Modern
Fireproof Construction, Fully
Insulated with Cross Ventilation,
Hot Water Heat, Private Tile
Showers, Hot and Cold Water,
Most Comfortable Beds.
17 inch Television. Open All Year.
Restaurant Near. *Prop.* A. E. Crisp."

Turnpike MOTEL

HWY. 73 N. J. S 41, ONE-HALF MILE WEST OF EXIT 4, ON NEW JERSEY TURNPIKE

Down
the River,
over
Creeks,
in the Pines

115

196

With a bog iron foundry and a
living history museum, Batsto is
located in the Wharton State Forest.
Munitions for Washington's
Continental Army were made here.
The water supply would have gone
to Philadelphia had it not been
for state law and New Jersey's
acquisition of the one hundred
thousand–acre stretch of pinelands
in 1954.

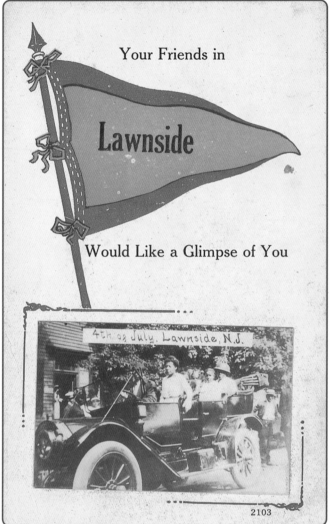

197

This reproduction postcard shows Elizabeth White, who is credited with cultivating blueberries that grew on the edge of her family's cranberry bogs. In 1916 she shipped the nation's first commercial batch to market. Along with Michigan and Oregon, New Jersey is one of the three leading states in the country to produce highbush (six-foot-tall) blueberries.

198

Settled by farmers and woodcutters in the late 1700s, Lawnside was a major stop on the Quaker-supported Underground Railroad during the Civil War. Located eight miles east of Camden, it was among the earliest African American towns to be incorporated in New Jersey. This car, which belonged to Emmett Rice, was photographed on Warwick Road.

199

Originally forty acres, the city was named after the earl of Camden, a colonial sympathizer. Its industrial growth and related role as an intermodal transportation hub began in 1834 when it became the terminus for the Camden & Amboy Railroad, built on the banks of the Delaware.

200

Good-bye cylinders. Hello platters. Millions of phonographic records were produced at this ten-acre plant before RCA Corporation acquired it. Long vacant, it is slated for condominium conversion.

201
This advertising postcard captures some of the glory days when Camden was a major port city.

202
"I must wait in this town 1 hr. for the electric train to Atlantic City. I am having a good time, so are the mosquoties [*sic*]," wrote a brother on August 17, 1915, to his sister back home in Lancaster, Pennsylvania.

203

This card is from an era when using the native son's name and image was a matter of civic pride and savvy marketing. The hotel is now empty.

204

On and off since the 1930s when it was first launched, the slogan "M'm! M'm! Good!" was the hoped-for reaction to the condensed soup invented at Second and Market Streets at the turn of the twentieth century by company chemist John T. Dorrance, who later became president of the company.

14:—BOAT RACES ON COOPER RIVER, CAMDEN, N. J.

48601

Colonial House, Haddonfield, N. J.
New Jersey changed from a Colony to a State by the Legislature in session here Sept. 1777.

205
The Cooper River bisects Camden, its banks providing grounds for a city park and a boat club. Annual rowing meets are held on the river named for the founding family of Camden.

206
Built in 1750, Indian King Tavern was the site of the first meeting of the New Jersey legislature in 1777. Today it is a museum that is part of a walking tour of historic Haddonfield.

207

A new zip code and town had to be carved out of Delaware Township after California developers opened the doors to Cherry Hill Mall.

208

One of the first racetracks to be built after state laws against betting on horse races were lifted, this track was completed by Eugene Mori in 1942. The property totals 223 acres. The clubhouse and grandstand had seating for twenty thousand people; its Luncheon Terrace served one thousand. There was parking for fifteen thousand cars. It was home to the Garden State and the Gardenia Stakes, two-year-old colt and filly championships, respectively, whose purses made them the wealthiest horse races in the country from the 1950s through the 1970s.

ON THE MALL AT CHERRY HILL

WOOLWORTH'S
CHERRY HILL GRILL

Garden State Park
Thoroughbred racing at its colorful best

THE HILL THEATRE, PAULSBORO, N. J.

209
This beautiful art deco theater in Paulsboro is still in use, though not as a movie house. Its interior is now used as a film studio.

210
The Pitman Grove Methodist Camp Meeting Association was established here between Alcyon Lake and Mantua Creek in Gloucester County in 1871. Summer residents from Camden and Philadelphia came via the West Jersey Railroad. The Summit Park Music Shell was dedicated on August 25, 1899. As more year-round residents moved in, the borough of Pitman was eventually organized in 1905.

211

One of the state's oldest Swedish settlements, the village was located on the stage line between Camden and Salem. For years it was a large shipping station for produce, notably tomatoes.

Lake Narraticon, Swedesboro, N. J.

212

Deepwater, a main junction for nearly half a dozen highways, would eventually become Exit 1 on the New Jersey Turnpike. Perfect place to put up a filling station—and a couple of industrial plants.

HAPPY MOTORING BEGINS AT CARLSON'S ESSO STATION INTERSECTION OF ROUTE 130 & 40, 2 MILES FROM PENNSVILLE FERRY COMPLETE LUBRICATION AND TUNE UP TEL PENNSGROVE 912 DEEPWATER, N.J.

ROLLER COASTER, RIVERVIEW BEACH, N. J.   92741

213
The endless loop of a roller coaster is portrayed in this one-time amusement park in Pennsville overlooking the Delaware.

Range Finder, Fort Mott, N. J.

214
Almost one hundred feet high, this range finder was used by cargo ships as a navigational aid to find the river's center channel. Fort Mott was built during the Civil War. It is the southern anchor site on the New Jersey Coastal Heritage Trail that begins here and goes around Cape May to Perth Amboy.

Broadway, Salem, New Jersey, showing Old Oak, Friends' Cemetery

We had some great times here: house-parties etc. 1/30/07 Guy.

Down
the River,
over
Creeks,
in the Pines

125

215

Founded by Quakers in 1675, this county seat three miles east of the Delaware
still has houses dating from the colonial era. The historic oak is located behind
the brick fence of the Friends Cemetery. It was once joked that it was four years older
than the Atlantic Ocean. Salem also was a site on the Underground Railroad.

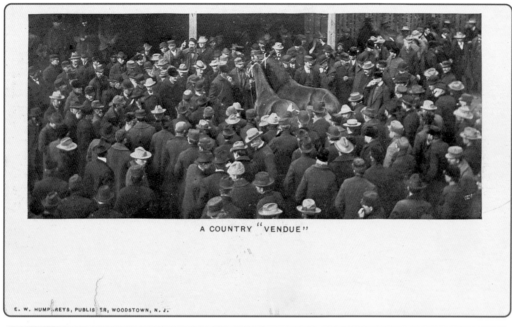

A COUNTRY "VENDUE"

E. W. HUMPHREYS, PUBLISHER, WOODSTOWN, N. J.

216

Dating back more than a century, weekly livestock and household auctions took place at Stony Harris's Sales Company on North Main Street in Woodstown. Here a horse auction—using the French word *vendue* for "sale"—is in progress.

S-34 HANCOCK HOUSE, BUILT 1734, SCENE OF REVOLUTIONARY MASSACRE, HANCOCK BRIDGE, N. J.

4A-H2192

217

Maintained by the state, the William and Sarah Hancock House is one of the better known examples of patterned brickwork in Salem County, with the owners' initials and date of construction woven into the western facade. Pension records of American Revolution veterans indicate that ten patriots were massacred in their sleep and five wounded by British troops here in 1778.

218

Apparently it also was an expensive day at the market, according to the postcard writer. Someone bought ten thousand dollars' worth of the spuds on October 9, 1905.

A BUSY DAY AT THE POTATO MARKET, ELMER, NEW JERSEY

219

The sun prepares to set over Penns Neck Bridge, spanning Salem Creek, near where the nuclear reactors are today.

Sunset on Salem Creek, towards Penna Neck Bridge, Salem, N.J.

Bay, Bounty, and Barrier Islands

SOUTHERN SHORE REGION

Think that all those urban colonists ever did was clear the land and build settlements? Well, according to a 1766 edition of the *Philadelphia Gazette,* they also took time off for health reasons. Their antidote? Sea bathing. Their travel destination? Cape May Island.

The conditions were pretty primitive by today's standards: nothing more than canvas tents. It took the Revolution and the rise of the gentry in Philadelphia to bring about the next phase in Cape May's evolution as a resort.

In 1801 Cape Island, as it was called, became the proverbial field of dreams for life-long resident and carpenter Ellis Hughes. "The situation is beautiful, just on the con-fluence of Delaware Bay with the Ocean in sight of the Light-house, and affords a view of the shipping which enters and leaves the Delaware. Carriages may be driven along the margin of the Ocean for miles; and the wheels will scarcely make any impression upon the sand, the slope of the shore is so regular that persons may wade out a great distance."

Hughes built a barnlike structure to accommodate overnight visitors. He called it a house room. At night, he dropped a sheet from the rafters in order to separate the men from the women. Hughes promised Philadelphians fish, oysters, crabs, good liquors, and access to lots of bathing in the salty brine. He put all of this in a newspaper advertisement in the *Aurora* that is generally regarded as the first of its kind to refer to Cape May as a seashore resort. Before listing the stage directions from Cooper's Ferry (Camden), he concluded with a flourish: "It is the most delightful spot the citizens can retire to in the hot season."

Breakfast and supper were listed at twenty-five cents each, dinner (the traditional noonday meal) at thirty-six-and-a-half cents, one night's lodging at seven cents, one gill of West India rum at ten cents, a sling of egg punch and a pint of Teneriffe wine at thirty-three cents each. One night stabling a horse with fresh hay was thirteen cents, but if you fed your horse the local salt hay, stabling was only seven cents. Then again, if you put the horse in the pasture instead of under cover, that, too, was only seven cents.

What a difference a couple of fires and changes in building styles have made.

By the 1890s architects were the royalty of construction, their ingenuity prized in all the different ways they used gables, brackets, dormers, slate roofs, observatory decks, porch pillars, fireplaces, and ornate railings on summer cottages, hotels, and boardinghouses, creating the Cape May we have today. Hughes's house room was long gone from the scene of hospitality. Not just in Cape May, either. The style spread up the Atlantic's barrier islands to Ocean City and westward along the fishing villages of the Delaware Bay and into Bridgeton.

Nobody practiced the real estate axiom "location, location, location" better than Charles K. Landis, a Philadelphia lawyer who arrived on the southern shore in 1861. Just four years earlier he had started a grape farm in Hammonton in Atlantic County. His field of dreams here was thirty-two thousand acres of wet, flat land he called Vineland. He designed a main thoroughfare (Landis Avenue) that was one hundred feet wide and proceeded to lay out a city one mile square around it. The avenues were planted with double rows of shade trees, and the residential setbacks were landscaped with azaleas and wisteria.

Landis, who also invested in a narrow-gauge railroad, sold buildings to would-be manufacturing entrepreneurs. In an attempt to bring farmers east to the affordable flat land he had for sale, he advertised in newspapers in the mid-Atlantic states. Still enamoured with the grape business, Landis convinced Italian immigrants to come to his agricultural utopia. But it was Dr. Thomas B. Welch, a local dentist, who came up with a method in 1869 that prevented grape juice from fermenting. His discovery was actually a solution to a more heavenly problem: its original intended use was for church Communion services.

Eventually the restless Landis turned his attention eastward to the barrier islands. In 1879 he bought Ludlam's Beach between Townsend and Corson's Inlets and tried to turn it into the Venice of the seashore. It came to be known as Sea Isle City.

Along what would become part of the East Coast's Intracoastal Waterway, other seashore resorts developed. The Baker Brothers—Latimer, Philip, and J. Thompson—from Lewisburg, Pennsylvania, went to work for Landis in Vineland, then went to the Atlantic coast to develop the Wildwood communities along Five Mile Beach. The West Jersey Railroad brought day-trippers here from the Camden station in trains that left after breakfast. Up to eight hours could be spent in the forested seascape before returning in time for dinner. These picnic excursions, as they were sometimes advertised, often included clambakes on the beach. The Wildwoods were also considered politically significant, drawing the attention of President Benjamin Harrison, who came for the Hotel Dayton dedication in 1890, and Governor Woodrow Wilson, who was a friend of J. Thompson Baker, by then a representative in the United States Congress.

Like the Wildwoods, the island of Ocean City was also designed by three brothers, only this fraternity was comprised of Methodist ministers who developed the Christian resort. Since 1897 Ocean City has been a dry town as a result of deed restrictions forbidding the sale or production of liquor, and, as such, it is a popular destination for families with small children. In addition to its boardwalk amusements and music pier, the city's main attractions include the storm-wrecked remains of the four-masted bark, *Sindia,* originally en route to New York from Japan with Christmas products.

Cape May and Cumberland Counties make up the Southern Shore region.

Herbert Bernstein, writing in *Vineland, N.J.: A Pictorial Review 1861–1921* in October 1975, observed, "The picture postcard performed a vital role in early twentieth century America and today is a much appreciated piece of nostalgia, well remembered by senior citizens and curiously looked at by younger generations."

220

Lafayette Street, Cape May, has been the welcome mat to the Southern Shore Region for years. It was a busy summer season in 1964 when, on July 3, the sender invited a friend back home in Blue Bell, Pennsylvania, to come attend the Cottager's Dinner Dance on July 18. "Everything is booming down here what with the ferry opening etc."

221

The S.S. *New Jersey* was one of the first four ferries bought to establish a travel route between Cape May Point and Lewes, Delaware. Ferry service was inaugurated on July 1, 1964.

222

Once a private home, this gingerbread Victorian cottage was bought in 1973 for one dollar and moved across the street so that a motel could be built on its original site. Now a gift shop, the building is located on the corner of Carpenters Lane and Perry Street.

LIGHT HOUSE. BY MOONLIGHT. CAPE MAY POINT. N. J.

60735

223

This is the third lighthouse to stand on Cape May Point overlooking Lily Pond; tides washed out the first two. Built in 1859 under the supervision of U.S. Army Corps of Engineers First Lieutenant George Gordon Meade, it stands 157 feet high, and its beam is visible up to twenty-four miles out at sea. It is surrounded by a 190-acre state park.

224

This concrete ship situated at the foot of Sunset Boulevard was one of an experimental group of ships built by the U.S. government during World War I because of the shortage of sheet metal. Promoters purchased the *Atlantus* for use as a ferry for a proposed route from Cape May Point to Lewes. One night a nor'easter broke it loose from its mooring, and it wound up listing at the foot of Sunset Beach, where very little of it is visible today.

CONCRETE SHIP ATLANTUS. CAPE MAY POINT. N. J.

62960

225

Survivors from prehistoric times, horseshoe crabs come ashore on the Delaware Bay every May, especially around Reeds Beach. In 1990 one million were counted; in 1999 four hundred thousand. Their eggs are food for the migratory red knots, sanderlings, and ruddy turnstones.

CAPE MAY AVENUE, WHITESBORO, N. J.

226

Whitesboro was established
as an all-black community on the
western side of the Cape May
peninsula in 1899. It was named for
North Carolina's George M. White,
an African American representative
in Congress during the post-
Reconstruction period. White
helped migrant workers find and
purchase the land in Cape May
County after a race riot in 1898
in Wilmington, Delaware.

227

Constructed in 1849 in the
Cape Cod style, East Point
Lighthouse in the Heislerville
section of Maurice River Township
was used as a navigational marker
by oyster schooners to the ports of
Mauricetown, Port Norris, Millville,
and Port Elizabeth. It is the second
oldest lighthouse in the state that
is still standing and inspired the
design of many of the early
lighthouses built along the
Pacific Coast.

228

The region's once-rich oyster history is preserved with the *A. J. Meerwald*, a restored 1928 Delaware Bay schooner docked at the remaining oyster sheds in Bivalve, part of Commercial Township in Cumberland County.

Unloading Oysters below Range Light, Bivalve, N. J.

229

The Weakfish Capital of the World: Fortescue remains a popular fishing resort, though most of the anglers come just for the day. The hotels and pavilions that once overlooked the bay are gone. In the 1930s the state purchased the marina.

AN AFTERNOON'S CATCH AT FORTESCUE, N.J.

Ledge Lighthouse, Delaware Bay, Off Fortescue, New Jersey.

230

Formally called the Elbow of Cross Ledge Lighthouse, this beacon fell in 1953 after a freighter loaded with ore struck it. The following year an automated light was mounted in its place.

Palace of Depression

VINELAND, NEW JERSEY, U.S.A

George Daynor — Originator, Designer and Builder

231

George Daynor arrived in Vineland broke in the fourth quarter of 1929. Wall Street had crashed and the Great Depression was on. Daynor "settled on an automobile dump in a mosquito-laden swamp" where "the ground was worth a dollar an acre." "Working alone and with only his two hands," Daynor built this eccentric castle out of clay and auto parts on four acres. It took him three years. When it was done, he charged ten cents to see it. What remained in the early 1970s was moved to Mill Road and is undergoing restoration.

232

Old Home Week in the summer of 1911 drew a throng of people, including J. A. Washburne, who brought with him his lap organ.

J. A. WASHBURNE
CO B 44 RE ? MASS.
AGE NEARLY 80
WITH HIS LAP ORGAN
MADE IN 1847.
THIS IS THE FIRST MUSICAL
INSTRUMENT USED IN THE
EARLY DAYS OF VINELAND.

SOUVENIR
OLD HOME WEEK
AUG. 6 TO 12, 1911
VINELAND N.J.

233

The first seeds to be sown in Vineland were for grapes.

BOARDWALK SCENE, ATLANTIC CITY, N. J.　　PUBLISHED by C. H. GRAVES

One of our permanent Advertising Stands. It will pay you to sell Vineland Grape Juice. Let us ship you a trial order.

VINELAND GRAPE JUICE COMPANY,　VINELAND, N. J.

1 CHICKEN FARM, VINELAND, N. J.   62372

234 & 235
Though named for the grapes that were cultivated here for twenty-five years, Vineland became known for its poultry farms, along with the fruits and vegetables grown on the outskirts of the one-square-mile city. Auctions were held daily.

Little Robin
Duck Farm,
Vineland, N. J.

236

Vineland's location in South Jersey made it a natural rail hub.

West Jersey R. R. Station.   Jersey Southern R. R. Station.

A 6391   Vineland, N. J.

Copyright 1905 by the Rotograph Co.

237

The Wheaton Museum of Glass in Millville is one of the top three glass museums in the country. Dr. T. C. Wheaton was a pharmacist who in 1884 turned to glass production. The museum is part of a re-created nineteenth-century village and studio where gaffers apprentice to learn how to blow glass.

6—View of Seabrook Farms, Bridgeton, N. J.

238

At the time this aerial photograph
was taken by Seabrook Farms as a
promotional postcard, "the world's
largest farming-freezing operation"
was processing vegetables from
its own nineteen thousand acres
plus the produce grown by 749
independent farmers. The yearly
output was seventy-five million
pounds of frozen food.

Tomato Wagons waiting to be unloaded at the
Canning Factory on Water Street, Bridgeton, N. J.

239

Bridgeton has been
a food-processing center
since the days of horse-drawn
wagons bringing the tomato
crop to town.

Along The Bank, Bridgeton, N.J. City Park, N.J.

240
A stock postcard promoting
"Cumberland County's Finest."

241
A bridge built across the creek in 1716 gave the hamlet
founded by Quakers its first name, Cohansey Bridge.
That name gave way to Bridge Town and then to Bridgeton,
the Cumberland County seat. The city park surrounds an old dam
built in 1814 to mark a millpond. Between Sunset Lake
and the edge of town is the raceway known locally
as the Northwest Passage, which attracts canoeists.

The House where the Tea was stored, Greenich, N. J.

242
The rallying cry of "No taxation without representation" was heard in South Jersey as well as in Boston. In December 1774 colonists angered by the arrival of a tea shipment broke into the house and carted the fragrant leaves to a bonfire in the public square. Two grand juries refused to convict the patriots, whose twenty-three names were subsequently inscribed on the granite monument.

GREENWICH, N. J. SEP. 30. — 08.

243
Proud patrons pose shortly after the stone marker commemorating the act of rebellion was unveiled in September 1908.

244

"The fish is fine."

245

This early-twentieth-century nighttime view is but a dim comparison to the Wildwood of today, where the blazon of neon lights seems to outshine even the patriotic fireworks.

Entrance to Wildwood Crest, N. J.

WILDWOOD CREST

SURFSIDE RESTAURANT

246 & 247
Altogether, the Wildwoods
comprise a five-mile-long
barrier island north of Cape May.
Wildwood Crest is the quietest of
the trio, which went from Victorian
gentility to the doo-wop of car
culture in less than forty years.

248

Built in 1897 at a cost of eighteen thousand dollars and later expanded, the Wildwood Casino boasted a two hundred–seat restaurant, a fifty–by–one hundred–foot dance floor that fronted a stage, 350 changing rooms with both robes and swimsuits for rent, hot sea water baths, fishing from the five hundred–foot pier for a nickel, a knickknack shop, a carousel, bowling alleys, billiard and Ping Pong tables, a basketball court, and, of course, a photo studio for souvenir postcards. It burned on August 4, 1964.

Casino, Wildwood, N. J.

249

Russian émigré Louis Sagel began selling taffy on the boardwalk in 1918. The business was later taken over, moved, and expanded by his son, Harry. It later became the Bella Vista restaurant. It burned on August 5, 1973.

Sagel's Original Salt Water Taffy, Poplar Avenue and Boardwalk, near the Ocean Pier, Wildwood, N. J.

Buckskin Bob—which toured with us through thirty states was probably one of the First Educated Horses ever featured on the American Stage.

This Picture was originally published in the New York Dramatic Mirror Christmas . . . 1900

Where's that fellow who said . . . "You haven't changed a bit." . . . The Liar . . .

The RossKams, Gertrude and C. H. R.
Now Retired on That Beautiful Island, in the Atlantic
Wildwood-by-the-Sea, N. J.

CHICAGO STOCK
SOUVENIR
POST CARD

PLACE STAMP HERE
DOMESTIC ONE CENT
FOREIGN TWO CENTS

CHAS. H. ROSSKAM MANAGER

This space may be used for Communication   This space for Address only

250

Many vaudeville, circus, theater performers, and movie actors, such as the RossKams, retired to New Jersey's various resorts, particularly amusement-driven ones on the Atlantic shore. The couple used this postcard at Christmas. The moniker "The Wildwoods by the Sea" came from a song written in 1905 by Lois Worden.

251

In 1907 Joseph M. Sweet built an enormous bathhouse on the boardwalk at Schellenger Avenue. It had three hundred changing rooms, locker rooms with showers for men, and a drying room that processed one thousand wet swimsuits an hour. A devastating fire on July 4, 1923, wiped out the entire operation.

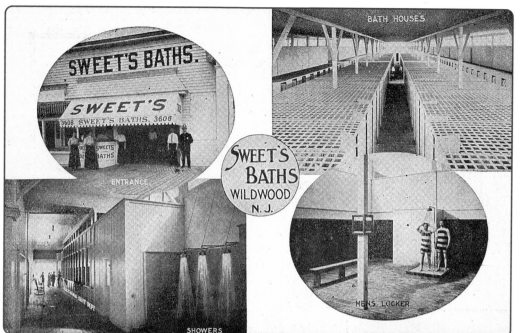

252

Dante? A dybbuk? The Jersey Devil? You decide. Thrill-seekers entered what was once called the Monster's Den for a spin on a "dark ride," the term used for enclosed roller coasters, on Mariner's Landing. It eventually was lost in a fire.

HOLLY BEACH LIFE SAVING CREW AND APPARATUS, HOLLY BEACH, N. J.

R.W. RYAN, WILDWOOD, N. J.

253
Founded in 1882 as Holly Beach, this section of Wildwood was one of the sites for the island's lifesaving stations.

6156

Copyright, 1906, Wildwood Post Card Co.

THE "HOLE DAM" FISH FAMILY RESIDE IN OTTEN'S CANAL, NORTH WILDWOOD, N. J 8-14.

J.B.R

254
In 1908 Henry Otten, according to one legend, stocked his canal on the western side of the island at Eighteenth Street and Delaware Avenue in North Wildwood with sea creatures and then inaugurated glass-bottomed boats for canal cruises.

255

The fishing village of Anglesea in North Wildwood is nearly equidistant from Great Egg Harbor and the mouth of the Delaware Bay, making Hereford Inlet a naturally occurring shelter from rough seas and the entry point for the Intracoastal Waterway. The Victorian-style Hereford Lighthouse began operation on May 11, 1874. It was placed on the National Register of Historic Places in 1977.

HEREFORD LIGHT, ANGLESEA, N.J.

256

Laid out as a residential travel destination in 1914, Stone Harbor is largely a family resort flanked by a bird sanctuary for herons and the Wetlands Institute.

STONE HARBOR, N. J.

Greetings From SEA ISLE CITY NEW JERSEY K 8347

Beach and Bathing View, America's Greatest Family Resort, Ocean City, N. J.

OCEAN CITY, N.J. DIAMOND JUBILEE 1954

K 7842

257

Ludlam Island was the original
name of this narrow, seven-mile
sand bar on which Stone Harbor
and Sea Isle City are located.
Each year female sea turtles
make their way from bay to ocean
across the island's busy main street
to lay their eggs.

258

Ocean City's enduring claim
as a family resort with an extensive
amusement-filled boardwalk and
music pier lies in the fact that it
is a dry town. Plus it has been
very clever in coming up with
promotional events centered
around such ubiquitous items
as crabs, french fries, and hats.

259

The grandest hotel on Ocean City's oceanfront, the Flanders was built in 1923.

260

You never know who you'll find gracing the front of a promotional postcard: 1950s pin-up queen Bettie Page poses at the right.

GREETINGS FROM OCEAN CITY, N. J.

Pass Go

GREATER ATLANTIC CITY REGION

In the fall of the 1976 political year, voter turnout all over New Jersey was crucial if a second attempt to rescue the economically depressed Atlantic City, and surrounding Atlantic County, was to succeed. The public question? Casino gambling. Two years earlier, a state constitutional referendum to legalize gambling throughout the Garden State failed. This time around, the question on the ballot limited the gambling to Atlantic City, with senior citizens as the beneficiaries.

The Committee to Rebuild Atlantic City received more than $1.2 million in contributions to push the referendum. Part of that money was spent just a few days before the November 2 ballot day, when thousands of thin paper postcards were sent to voters as reminders to go to the polls. The referendum passed by a two hundred thousand–vote margin. And, as the saying goes, the rest is history.

Though postcards played a last-minute role in helping to decide Atlantic City's future, they have played a part in promoting the one-time world-famous health resort and its neighboring communities since the late nineteenth century. It began with a trip to Europe in 1895. According to deltiologist and radio personality Ed Davis writing in *Atlantic City Diary: 1880–1985*, Mrs. Carl Voelker returned from visiting family in her native Germany to tell her husband she had an idea for diversifying his printing business. The rage at European resorts was writing messages on little cards whose fronts had pictures on them. Some were scenic vistas. Some were of fancy hotels. Some were cards with posies and simple verse. Wherever she went, she saw people writing brief words of salutation and posting the little missives in the mail. In fact, vacationers had been doing this since 1869, when the first postcard was sent in Austria.

Carl Voelker was already publishing a German-language newspaper that went out to the émigré community. So, reasoned his wife, why not print postcards that they and visitors to Atlantic City could send home? Why not approach the local hotels with the suggestion of using postcards to advertise their beachfront presence? What resulted caused Atlantic City to become New Jersey's most prodigious producer of postcards. "Colorful picture post cards of Atlantic City hotels, piers, and boardwalk were available at many locations, but one of the largest selections of cards was that at Frank B. Hubin's Big Post Card Store, 813 Boardwalk," Davis notes.

261
Easter Sunday March 27, 1910.
Postmarked two days later,
the card's sender wrote:
"Today is an ideal summer day
and we have been outdoors all day."

Tourists were coming to the Queen of Resorts in droves from Philadelphia, New York, Pittsburgh, and Washington, D.C. The city vied with Saratoga Springs, New York; Hollywood, Florida; and even with resorts in California and Europe for the travel trade. At the same time, it found regional competition from Asbury Park to the north and the Wildwoods to the south.

In 1914 Atlantic City touted itself as "the premier pleasure and health resort of America." The boast wasn't far off the mark. It was Mendham physician Dr. Jonathan Pitney who convinced Philadelphia and South Jersey entrepreneurs to invest in a railroad to bring the masses to Absecon Island in 1854 where he, not coincidentally, also had a practice. Using real estate to sell real estate, the streets and avenues in the gridded city were given names from all around the United States—an idea reinvented in the Depression-era board game Monopoly, which endures in popularity. And the more people came to Atlantic City, the more the descendents of the original farmers were pushed farther out into Atlantic County.

Smaller health resorts developed outside Atlantic City, notably in Egg Harbor City. Farms, which supplied the hotel restaurants, shared space with livestock, including thoroughbred horses, which provided resort visitors with a couple of different sporting venues, as did fishing. The golfing craze also took hold and grew.

Since the inauguration of casino gambling, Atlantic City has come to be regarded by many out-of-state visitors taking a bus to get here as a sort of city-state. Yet it is the whole of Atlantic County that makes up the Greater Atlantic City Region.

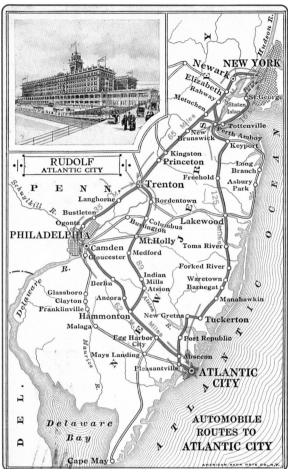

262

Icons in chrome: the Absecon lighthouse, precasino hotels,
and the rolling chairs on the boardwalk. The herringbone pattern
on the boardwalk is for pedestrians, while the lengthwise wood
is to help make it easier to push the rolling chairs.

263

This hotel advertising card shows the best
auto routes to Atlantic City from Philadelphia
and New York. Located across from the
Garden Pier at New Jersey Avenue,
the Rudolf became the Breakers,
a kosher hotel, in 1916.
It was torn down in 1974.

WHARF AT LONGPORT TRANSFER POINT FOR
OCEAN CITY BOATS

Scene along lines of Atlantic City & Shore Railroad, between Atlantic City and Ocean City

264
With Ocean City firmly grounded
as a religious resort, vacationers
who wanted more excitement could
take the shuttle boats north across
Great Egg Harbor Inlet to Longport
and there catch the trolley to
Atlantic City.

MISS AMERICA

265
Threatened by the competition
for tourist dollars that the
annual Asbury Park Baby Parade
commanded, Atlantic City launched
the Miss America Beauty Pageant
in 1921.

266

Atlantic City had a vibrant African American community that, as the twentieth century got under way, included entertainment revues, as seen in this card postmarked 1903.

267

Opened in 1898 at Virginia Avenue, the Steel Pier was built for two hundred thousand dollars. The amusement pier eventually became known as a talent showcase for a wide variety of entertainers and novelty acts. Comedians Abbott and Costello, singers Frank Sinatra and Sophie Tucker, and big band leaders Tommy Dorsey and Harry James appeared here. In 1934 horse-diver Arnette Webster French rode the waves with Rex.

DIVING HORSE, OCEAN END STEEL PIER, ATLANTIC CITY, N. J.—75

268

In 1905 Lorena Carver, daughter of a Wild West showman, took up her father's act. "All the girl has to do is look pretty and not fear height or water," Carver once said. "The horse knows what to do." Both the act and the pier closed in 1978.

STEEPLE CHASE PIER, ATLANTIC CITY, N. J.—49A

269

Coney Island impresario George Tilyou headed to Atlantic City in 1904 and opened up Steeplechase Pier, a similar amusement park at Virginia Avenue. In addition to the various thrill rides, patrons could also rent clown costumes to wear. Seen here in the early 1950s, the signature grinning face is the likeness of Tilyou's brother.

270

Built in 1913 with formal flower beds and the Keith Vaudeville Theater at its eastern end, the partially reconstructed Garden Pier today is home to the Atlantic City Historical Museum and the Florence Valore Miller Art Gallery.

271

Seven acres of concrete between Georgia and Mississippi Avenues, Convention Hall opened in 1929 without roof posts and pillars. The cavernous interior was tall enough to fly a helicopter in and deep enough that Yankee baseball slugger Mickey Mantle could hit a home run.

AEROPLANE RETURNING TO BEACH AFTER FLIGHT ALONG OCEAN FRONT, ATLANTIC CITY, N. J.

HOTEL HYGEIA
ATLANTIC CITY, N. J.
NEW YORK AVENUE, NEAR BEACH AND AMUSEMENTS
ALBERT M. HOCHSTADTER, PROP.
European Plan 50c, 75c, $1.00 per day. Special Weekly Rates.
Electric Lights, Steam Heat, Metal Beds, 40-lb. Hair Mattresses.
Rooms with Bath   Everything Modern. Open All year.
Popular Price Restaurant. Bathing Permitted from House.
The Leading Popular Price European Plan House with rates
the same Summer and Winter.

272
People in Atlantic City have had a fascination with aeronautics
ever since flying fever swept the country in the early part of
the twentieth century. Airborne machines such as this seaplane
provided vacationers with yet another outlet for thrills.

273
This early-twentieth-century hotel postcard
advertised some the era's amenities.
The hotel took its name from the
Greek goddess of health.

274 & 275
Guess what year?
Roundtrip bus fare was $4.05,
plus tax. The Allegheny Commuter
cost a little more.

Hygeia Baths—Ocean and Pool Bathing, Hot and Cold Sea Water Tub Baths.
Rhode Island Avenue and Boardwalk, above Heinz's Pier, Atlantic City, N. J.
Open all Year, Day and Night. Water Pumped Constantly from Ocean.

Sun & Star Roof (Daytime) · The SENATOR, Atlantic City, N. J.

276 & 277
Built in 1910, the Hygeia Baths
were patronized by health
aficionados who were either
day-trippers, residents, or staying
at hotels that didn't have a
swimming pool. Forty years later
health trends changed. The rooftop
tanning salon on South Carolina
Avenue boasted "sunshine every
day regardless of the weather
outdoors with banks of scientific
sun-lamps, infrared, ultraviolet
and RS reflector, duplicating the
three components of sunshine—
light, warmth and energy."

278

Writing on May 5, 1912, the vacationer confesses, "Have thought of you many times, but I write very little." The spacious rolling chair design was adapted from wheelchairs. Originally meant to give those with infirmities the benefit of fresh air, the chairs were modified for the other tourists who clamored to use them.

279

Purely for promotional purposes, the H. J. Heinz Company of Pittsburgh bought the Iron Pier on Massachusetts Avenue in 1898 and converted it into an exhibition space where the company gave away sample products and a little pickle souvenir pin. The pier was razed in 1945 following the devastating hurricane of 1944.

THE PEANUT STORE
1011 BOARDWALK, ATLANTIC CITY, N. J.

280

Just like the Heinz 57 Varieties, Planters Peanuts gave tourists an idea of all the different ways to eat goobers. An employee wore the monocled Mr. Peanut costume to draw customers into the shop at Virginia Avenue.

MILTON LATZ' KNIFE AND FORK INN, ATLANTIC CITY, N. J.   J.F.

281

Built in 1912 as a private men's club in Atlantic City's southern Chelsea section, this Flemish-style building is the focal point at the intersection of Albany and Pacific Avenues and has defied attempts to be obliterated by the wrecking ball. In 1927 the Latz family took it over and, four generations later, still run it.

282

Saltwater taffy was born in Atlantic City in the aftermath of a storm that swept through a boardwalk taffy store. Or so the legend goes. Philadelphian Joseph Fralinger, who began his boardwalk career with juice, fruit, and candy stands, hit on the idea of packaging the candy in boxes that vacationers could take home instead of the nickel bags that merely satisfied an impulse.

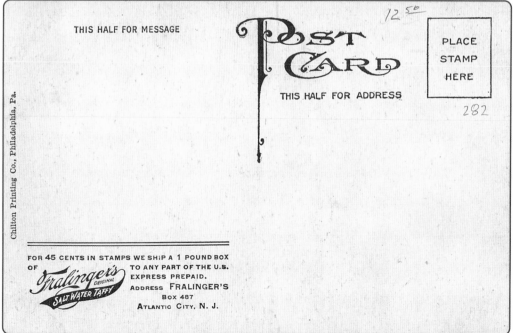

Lobster King Harry Hackney with his Lobster Waitresses who won the Prize in Atlantic City's Famous Beauty Pageant Parade on the Atlantic City Boardwalk

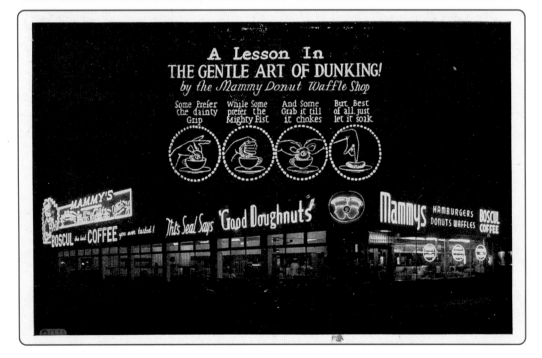

A Lesson In
THE GENTLE ART OF DUNKING!
by the Mammy Donut Waffle Shop

Some Prefer the dainty Grip

While Some prefer the Mighty Fist

And Some Grab it till it chokes

But Best of all just let it soak

283
Harry Hackney, another colorful Atlantic City promoter, had a lobster seafood restaurant that could seat three thousand diners at once. He posed here with his costumed waitresses, whom he dressed up as the red crustaceans, putting them in the Miss America parade in the 1940s.

284
In 1882 electricity came to Atlantic City. By 1908 the boardwalk at night was a blaze of electric art work. Mammy's was located on Pennsylvania Avenue as part of Steeplechase Pier.

285 & 286

This postcard urged voters
to go to the polls on November 2,
1976, and pull the lever for "yes"
to bring legalized gambling
to the ailing Queen of Resorts.
Chalfonte-Haddon Hall was
the first hotel on the East Coast
to put in a casino. It opened
its doors as Resorts International
on May 26, 1978.

DENNIS FARM DELICACIES DELIGHT HOTEL DENNIS DINERS — *in Atlantic City, N. J.*

287 & 288
From bounty to boardwalk:
beyond the city limits, farmland
rolled westward in Atlantic County.
These postcards show how the
Hotel Dennis promoted its cuisine.
The hotel was located on
Michigan Avenue.

HOTEL DENNIS DINING ROOM -- FAMED FOR ITS OWN FARM FOODS — *in Atlantic City, N. J.*

289

West meets East as a Trenton institution sets up shop on the Atlantic City boardwalk to sell slices of its spicy porcine product.

290

Lucy, the ninety-ton tin pachyderm, has been used to sell real estate from its six-story-high howdah, as a dance hall located in its stomach, as a gimmick to draw hotel guests to the Elephant Hotel at its feet, and most recently as a museum dedicated to its oceanfront history. Lucy has gazed out at the ocean since 1881.

WORLD FAMOUS DUDE RANCH
On the Boardwalk in Atlantic City

THEY'RE OFF! ATLANTIC CITY RACE TRACK, MAYS LANDING, N.J.

291, 292, & 293

Atlantic City and horses have been synonymous since the giddy-up. Horses were used to promote the resort's R&R benefits to the armed services' air divisions during World War II and as a noncity betting opportunity before the casinos came. There was even an "after-dark" nightspot, "Way Out West on the 'Walk,'" on Connecticut Avenue.

HORSEBACK RIDING AND CYCLING ALWAYS POPULAR

294
Begun in 1855 to serve the needs of the city's growing Italian American community, St. Nicholas of Tolentino Roman Catholic Church outgrew its two previous addresses before parishioners built this beautifully intricate marble edifice at Pacific and Tennessee Avenues.

ST. NICHOLAS CHURCH, ATLANTIC CITY—21

THE JERSEY DEVIL
mixing his favorite brew

295

Sometimes called the Leeds Devil after its
alleged birthplace near Smithville, this creature
of folklore, with its batlike wings, cloven hoofs,
horns, animal face, and forked tale,
is supposed to be the child of a witch who
cursed her thirteenth child to be born a devil.
From the name of an ice hockey team
to the imprint on a highly collectible
medicinal bottle, the Jersey Devil is a permanent
part of the state's cultural landscape.

296

A general store was moved to Smithville as part of a plan
launched in the early 1950s by Absecon antique dealers
Fred and Ethel Noyes to preserve historic buildings in South Jersey.
About thirty buildings, including a gristmill, barbershop, log cabin,
and Quaker meetinghouse, were reconstructed on land surrounding
the 1787 Smithville Inn located on Route 9.

297

Boasting two eighteen-hole golf courses instead of the original twenty-seven-hole course, this country club and conference center is run by the Marriott Corporation as a luxury resort nine miles north of Atlantic City.

SEAVIEW COUNTRY CLUB
ABSECON · NEW JERSEY

298

E. Hornberger's Bakery in Pleasantville once invited patrons to "Try our Cinnamon Buns."

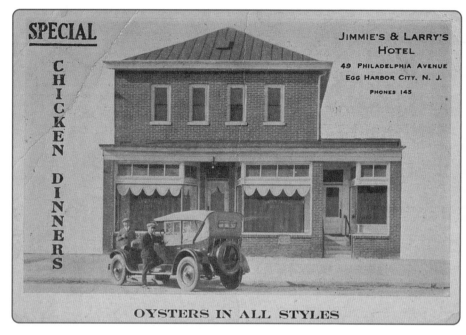

Renault Vineyards — Since 1864

Renault's Famous Hospitality Center

299
A speakeasy during Prohibition, the restaurant burned down
sometime around World War II. The back reads in pencil:
"Jimmy Gold Tooth/Larry Bald Head."

300
Louis N. Renault, emissary for
the duc de Montebello, found himself
stranded in America at the outbreak of the
Franco-Prussian War. Finding South Jersey's
temperate climate and soil ideal for growing
grapes, in 1870 he started the family's vintner
business in Egg Harbor City.

301

The good doctor rerouted a local creek into a serpentine configuration and had his patients walk against the water flow in summer and in winter (they wore wool garments). In addition to exercise in the cedar-colored water, Smith believed in fresh air and no alcohol. His sanitarium burned to the ground in 1928. City hall and the city's museum now occupy the London Avenue property.

DR. SMITH' SANITARIUM

PUBL BY H.KIRSCHT
EGG HARBOR CITY, N. J.

EGG HARBOR CITY, N J

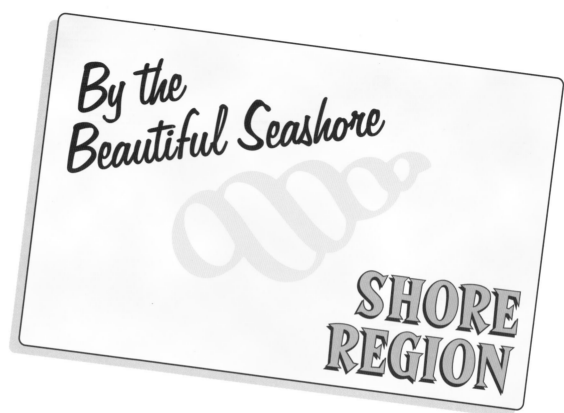

By the
Beautiful Seashore

SHORE
REGION

The endless expanse of ocean. High bluffs and low bays. A rambling landscape of oak, pine, beach plum, and soft sand. All the fish and clams you could harvest. No wonder the Lenapes loved the shore.

Apparently, Elliston Perot did so as well. This Philadelphian came to Long Branch in 1788 and rented a room in a farmhouse. When Perot asked if he could bring his wife with him the following year, the farmer suggested that the city slicker also bring his own bedding. Within a few short years Perot was part of a real estate syndicate that bought out the farmer. They turned his dwelling, located in the general vicinity of Ocean and Bath Avenues today, into a rooming house, put up a shingle, and started advertising the accessibility to healthy salty sea water.

Time progressed, as did the resort. The change in Shore tourism traffic from Philadelphians to New Yorkers was influenced partly by an anonymous 1809 letter to the *New York Herald.* The writer started by explaining, "Four years ago I took a trip to Long Branch, a bathing place on the shore of the Atlantic sea, chiefly resorted to by the opulent citizens of Philadelphia. . . . I was then much pleased with the . . . respectability and sobriety of the company resorting thither; the majority of whom, I was persuaded, came for the improvement of their health, and relaxation from the cares of business, at the most leisure season of the year, rather than to spend their money and time in dissipation—falsely called pleasure!

"I could not then help thinking it a pity that this inviting place was not more known and resorted to by the New Yorkers, being a little more than fifty miles from our city, whilst the Philadelphians have to travel nearly eighty miles to it."

At least two young New Yorkers came, according to the 1941 comparative account of Newport, Narragansett, Saratoga Springs, Long Branch, and Bar Harbor by Richmond Barrett in *Good Old Summer Days*. Barrett had interviewed a Mrs. John King Van Rensselaer, who recounted to him how a little boy named Teddy Roosevelt once knocked out her front tooth on the Long Branch beach.

Eight presidents vacationed here. The cigar-loving Ulysses S. Grant started the tradition of a summer White House in New Jersey in 1869 and regularly returned through 1884. James Garfield died here. His vice president who succeeded him, Chester Arthur, loved to bet on the ponies at Eatontown's Monmouth Park. Benjamin Harrison, when he wasn't in Wildwood, hobnobbed here with his north shore constituents, staying at the Elberon Hotel, as did Rutherford B. Hayes, who seems to have kept a low profile. William McKinley's vice president, Garret A. Hobart, was born in neighboring West Long Branch and when in office had a summer home in town where McKinley stayed. Woodrow Wilson accepted his party's renomination in 1916 at an estate whose name, Shadow Lawn, would be part of the title of a scathing attack on Wilson by the politically aspiring former president Theodore Roosevelt, who criticized Wilson's supposed softness concerning Germany's submarine activities.

Long Branch itself would be assailed by a politician. Asbury Park founder, the moralistic James A. Bradley, was elected to the state assembly where in 1894 he pushed through a bill banning gambling in New Jersey. What went was not only horse-racing and betting parlors but also the glittering crowds of New York's gossip world: Lillie Langtry, Diamond Jim Brady, and Lillian Russell. Even author Mark Twain retreated from the shore. In response to the effects of Bradley's heavy hand, a young Stephen Crane lampooned the new York brush maker in his summer dispatches on Asbury Park for metropolitan newspapers.

The twin resorts of Asbury Park and Ocean Grove, separated only by a slim lagoon filled with brackish water, offered a unique blend of old-time religious renewal and secular leisure. Asbury Park started the East Coast's first Baby Parade. Listed on the National Register of Historic Places, Ocean Grove still rolls out the welcome mat for summer religious revivals.

The Shore is also more than just sandy oceanfront and rivers filled with pleasure boats. Its boundaries extend deep into the state's coastal plain, where the Garden State still exists, New Jerseyeans love of horses is still seen, and leisure time is still spent in a different way than at the immediate shoreline.

"Fall would be here before we knew it. With pickin' up hick'ry nuts, cranberries and apples; and there'd be Harvest Moon corn huskin' parties with music and games and more good things to eat," Lillian M. Lopez wrote in her semiautobiographical account of growing up in Waretown in the late 1800s. "Oft'times of an evenin' when the weather was fit, after the supper things was put away, I'd walk with Jenny down to the bay. . . . As we trotted along we talked about when Pete was home and that time he hired a wagon and took us all to Toms River to see the circus train. It was so exciting; about forty railroad cars full of animals I'd only seen in picture books and never thought I would see for real."

In 1973 Great Adventure was constructed in Jackson Township. When it opened its doors, the amusement park with a drive-through saafari changed tourism in New Jersey. Great Adventure's creator, New York restaurant impresario Warner LeRoy, successfully shifted focus away from cramped urban zoos and boardwalk amusements to a seemingly limitless parklike compound with all-day and all-night entertainment, unmetered parking, and one general admission price.

Monmouth and Ocean Counties make up the Shore Region.

302
From hotel to hydrofoil: this bayside location in Highlands has been hospitable to travelers
since the late nineteenth century when it was Connor's Cedar Grove Hotel.
In the 1950s Connor's became a popular cabana club and restaurant.
It was sold to make way for the New York Fast Ferry.

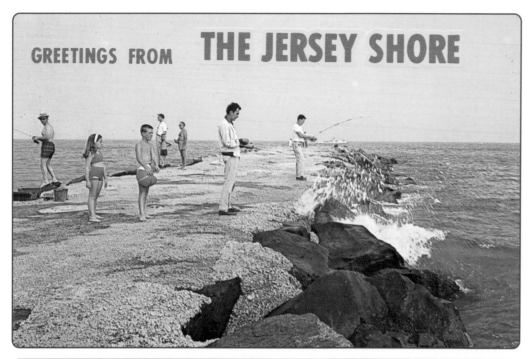

GREETINGS FROM **THE JERSEY SHORE**

303

Alternately reviled and championed for the sand they divert and deposit, the jetties designed by the U.S. Army Corps of Engineers are a permanent fixture along the 127 miles that make up the state's Atlantic shoreline from Sandy Hook to Cape May Point. Less destructible than wooden piers, they are popular with those who fish.

HENDRICK HUDSON SPRINGS, ATLANTIC HIGHLANDS, N. J.

304

A freshwater spring, a pipe, and a little marketing magic gave birth to the Henry Hudson Springs in 1830 when Louis Desperaux began charging ship captains five cents a barrel for the water.

305 & 306

New York merchants chipped in to build America's first lighthouse as a beacon
to help guide their ships into New York harbor. It was built in 1763 on what was then
the tip of Sandy Hook. This view dates from the 1920s. Named for Civil War General
Winfield S. Hancock, Fort Hancock, with its disappearing gun turrets, guarded the harbor
during three wars: the Spanish-American War and World Wars I and II.

The Lighthouse, Highlands, N. J.

307
With Sandy Hook about 250 feet below, Beacon Hill in Highlands was the more logical site for a semaphore station. In 1862 a permanent fortresslike structure was built with brownstone quarried from Belleville. One square tower and one round tower give it the name Twin Lights.

DIRECTLY ON THE OCEAN

308
Once a tiny fishing village on a barrier beach, Sea Bright blossomed in the 1890s as a fashionable resort between Sandy Hook and Long Branch. The last oceanfront hotel from the Victorian era, the Peninsula House fell victim to a mysterious fire in 1985.

AERIAL VIEW OF PENINSULA HOUSE   SEA BRIGHT, NEW JERSEY

309

The Navesink River has long been a popular venue for ice boating.

ICE BOAT RACING, RED BANK, N. J.

57335

310

The buildings remain, but their uses have changed. The Strand Theater and J. J. Newberry sites are occupied by Merrill Lynch, and a financial services concern has offices in the Whitfield Building. The cupola is gone, and instead of liquors, antiques are sold from the corner building. The white granite bank building now houses Smith Barney.

BROAD STREET, RED BANK, N. J.

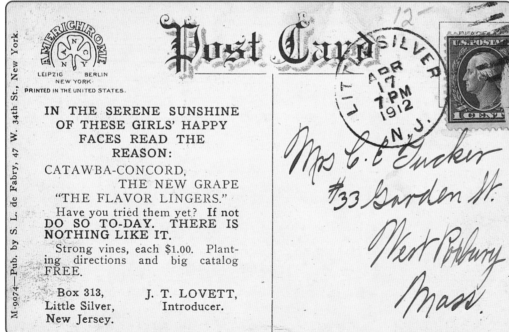

311

A postcard advertising the results of what you might reap if you bought from the nursery stock of J. T. Lovett.

312

With the store addition to the right removed, the Allen House was restored by the Monmouth County Historical Association. The building is located at the historic four-corners intersection of Broad Street and Sycamore Avenue in Shrewsbury.

...orner Store.   Shrewsbury N. J.
This is an old house standing here during the Revolution. The store is still in use. When we lived in Eatontown you passed this home on the way to Red Bank. I am having a fine rest, but too short - only a week. Lovely country. Hope you are well affectionate Lelia

313

Used as a base for the U.S. Signal Corps in World War I, Camp Vail was where engineers outfitted airplanes with radio communications, but not this craft used from a stock photo pool. In 1925 the camp was renamed Fort Monmouth after a pivotal battle in the American Revolution.
It was originally named in honor of Samuel F. B. Morse's partner, Alfred Vail.

Copyright I. F. S.

HANLEY-PAGE BOMBING MACHINE.   GREETINGS FROM CAMP VAIL, N. J.

"ON THE TURN", Monmouth Park Race Track, Oceanport, N. J.

314

In the late 1930s, in anticipation that pari-mutuel wagering would be allowed, the Monmouth Park Jockey Club was founded in Oceanport by a group of investors that included Amory Haskell, Philip Iselin, and Joseph Roebling. The track opened for business on June 19, 1946. A year later its clubhouse, visible from the Atlantic Ocean, was completed.

A RAMBLE THROUGH THE PARK
PLEASURE BAY,
LONG BRANCH, N.J.

Arthur Livingston, Publisher, New York 566

315

Long Branch was entertaining a nation not only on its beaches but also on the banks of the South Shrewsbury River. As the new twentieth century dawned, this forested amusement park had all the high-spirited entertainment that the more staid Asbury Park did not. Pleasure Bay apartments occupy the site today.

316

The hurricane of 1944 spiraled up New Jersey's coast, leaving millions of dollars of resort wreckage in its path.

What's left of Merry-Go-Round on Long Branch, N. J. Pier, Hurricane Sept. 14, 1944

317

Long Branch and the nation mourned the death of President James Garfield in 1881. After being shot, Garfield was brought here by a private rail spur built during the night to his favorite seaside cottage. The structure is no longer standing.

Franklin Cottage, in which President Garfield died, Elberon, N. J.

THE SUMMER CAPITAL

Spacious are thy halls, O! Shadow Lawn,
Where grey and silent creeps the quiet dawn,
A thing of beauty, clothed in dignity,
Shadow Lawn "The White House-by-the-sea"

Copyright Feb. 1916

CHARLOTTE L. COBB,
Long Branch, N. J.

MURRAY GUGGENHEIM COTTAGE, WEST END, N. J.

318 & 319

President Woodrow Wilson ran his reelection campaign from this estate. Actually located in West Long Branch, the property was later acquired by Hubert Parsons, F. W. Woolworth Company president, in his bid to be a part of Shore society. One of his neighbors was Murray Guggenheim, heir to a Colorado mining fortune. The Parsons property succumbed to fire, and a new mansion was built in its place. Today both estates are part of Monmouth University.

320

In 1890 Asbury Park launched the first Baby Parade on the East Coast. The annual August event drew upward of ten thousand visitors to the resort, which vied with Atlantic City for tourism dollars. Contestants were judged on their floats and costumes, each more intricately elaborate than the next.

Group of Prize Winners
ASBURY PARK, N.J.

321

Ida Jacobs opened a fast-food stand in 1922 that her daughter, Jeanette Weiner, continued. In the early 1970s the corner building was bought by a brief succession of hopeful entrepreneurs, one of whom turned it into a rock club he named the Stone Pony. As a result of the musical legends that sprang up around Bruce Springsteen's performances here, the club has a permanent place in rock 'n' roll history.

MRS. JAY'S BAR AND GRILL — OCEAN AND SECOND AVENUES — ASBURY PARK, NEW JERSEY   5A-H1673

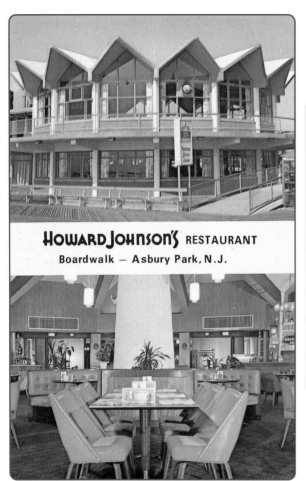

SAND STATUE, ASBURY PARK, N. J.

WANTED
Men to worK in
PIE FACTORY
$10 Per Day

322

In 1963 Asbury Park rebuilt many
of the concessions on its boardwalk, including
this gem of doo-wop architecture that is the last
Howard Johnson's in New Jersey.

323

In the early years of the twentieth century African American artist
Lorenzo Harris Sr. left the crowded and competitive sand-art scene
of Atlantic City for a better opportunity in Asbury Park.
With a mercantile license from the city, Harris, who had one arm,
practiced his art at the whites-only beach at the foot of First Avenue
with the help of his young son, who carried pails of water from the sea.
At least one of his sand sculptures found its way onto a postcard.

324

"The Place for Gracious Living" is how the Hotel Carver just over the Asbury Park border in Neptune promoted itself circa 1950. At the time, it was one of only a few Shore hotels to cater to African Americans. The back of the postcard indicates a "Beautiful Dining Room, Bar and Grill, Spacious Lawn, Croquet, Cards, Checkers, and Bathing on the Asbury Park Beach. Make reservations early." In later years the hotel became a rooming house. It sustained a fire in 2000.

325

Childhood memories are made of this: fairy-tale villages for the very young. Storyland Village on the Asbury Park traffic circle in Neptune was a fifty-acre theme park based on *A Child's Garden of Verses* and other stories. This postcard depicts Jack the Giant Killer from "Jack and the Beanstalk." A shopping plaza is on the site today.

NO SUNDAY DRIVING
OCEAN GROVE, N. J.

326

From its beginning in 1870 the Ocean Grove Methodist Camp Meeting Association forbade the driving vehicles of any kind within its borders on Sundays. But on June 22, 1979, the state supreme court ruled that the city's government violated the Constitution's separation of church and state, and driving on Sundays has been legal ever since.

Ocean Grove Auditorium, Ocean Grove, N. J.

327

The core of Ocean Grove, which is listed on the National Register of Historic Places, surrounds the Great Auditorium. This mammoth wood structure was built in 1894. The flag was added as a patriotic touch during World War I.
A special key in the Robert Hope-Jones organ console activates lights in the flag to create the illusion that it is waving in a breeze. It was slated to be replaced with a smaller, removable flag.

328

From Laura Ashley decor to more spartan interiors reminiscent of a bygone era, these canvas tents have been the summer homes of five generations of vacationing Methodists.

329

Popular with trendsetting Wall Street denizens, Spring Lake has always drawn a fashionable crowd, as much from Philadelphia as from New York. St. Catharine's Roman Catholic Church is the Roman Renaissance-baroque homage of the Maloney family to a daughter, seventeen, who died from tuberculosis in 1900. The architect was Horace Trumbauer of Philadelphia.

Spring Lake, N. J.,
St. Catherine's Catholic Church from across the Lake.

WORLD
LONGES
BAR

THE WORLD'S LONGEST BAR

At the New

OSPREY HOTEL

MANASQUAN BEACH, N. J.

Serving the finest wines and liquors, the Osprey Bar is
the mecca of all vacationists to the North Jersey Shore.
By actual measurement and comparison, the longest bar
in the universe! If you were to occupy one of its com-
fortably upholstered stools each night, it would take you
4 months and 23 days to do so . . . and every minute
most enjoyable.

Date of Visit..., 19.......

Mixologist in
Attendance ....

Entertained by ....

I HEARTILY RECOMMEND THAT YOU VISIT THE
OSPREY ON YOUR NEXT VISIT TO THE SHORE.

Signed..

Pub. by Noumain Studios, Asbury Park, N. J.   63312

Dextone · Made Direct from Kodachrome and Ansco Color. By Dexter Press, Pearl River, N. Y.

4.

POST CARD

Address

PLACE

STAMP

HERE

330

Drinking at the "World's Longest
Bar," a venerable watering hole,
is a rite of passage for many
attaining the age of majority.

331

Originally built in 1896 to break up the forty-mile gap of darkness between Barnegat and Twin Lights, this tidy Victorian lighthouse was decommissioned in 1945. It is now a museum.

Sea Girt Lighthouse
Sea Girt, N. J.

JC-H1578

332

Our House Tavern is starting its fourth century but with a different phone number.

OUR HOUSE TAVERN — Starting Its Third Century — Since 1747
This quaint old tavern is located in Farmingdale, N. J., between Freehold and all Jersey Shore Points. Enjoy a delicious Turkey, Chicken, Duck, Guinea Hen or Steak dinner here in an hospitable atmosphere of comfort and refinement.   Our Bar is a favorite rendezvous for those who know fine Liquors Closed Mondays Except Holidays — Open All Year — Dinner Served 12 to 9 P.M. — Tel. WEbster 8-6811

Gateway to the deserted Village of Allaire near Lakewood, N.J.   May 21/07

333
James Allaire of New York
bought the Howell Works in 1822
and turned it into a successful
iron-making operation that
supplied the air chambers for
Robert Fulton's steamship *Clermont*
and water pipes for New York City.
The once-thriving company town,
complete with church, mill, general
store, school, and dwellings, has
been restored and is a state park.

MOLLY PITCHER WELL, FREEHOLD, N. J.

MOLLY PITCHER WELL

334
One of the earliest made-up tourist
attractions, circa 1940: one of three
wells where Molly Hays was alleged
to have drawn water to slake the
thirst of Revolutionary War soldiers
fighting in the Battle of Monmouth.

335

This postcard advertises the historic American Hotel in Freehold by appealing to the horse-racing fans that patronize Freehold Raceway, a harness track located less than a mile away.

VISIT OUR

GRILL

ROOM

"The Horsiest Place in New Jersey"

336

The colonial York Road from the Amboys to Burlington was known as Main Street where it crossed through Allentown. Still standing today, this hotel was one of four inns in the bustling town named after Nathan Allen, who built three mills on the York Road.

Hotel, Allentown, N. J.

337
The original salesroom on Route 537 in the Scobeyville section of Colts Neck was simply an addition to a barn, as seen here in the late 1950s. The barn today is part of the Eastmont Orchards, while Delicious Orchards is located down the road on Route 34, where it is a full-service food emporium.

338
A daring concept to suburban audiences when it opened in June 1968, this 5,058-seat amphitheater at Telegraph Hill Park on the Garden State Parkway was designed by architect Edward Durell Stone, who went on to design the Kennedy Center in Washington, D.C. Currently it is known as the PNC Bank Center.

339

Catching a marlin off the coast of New Jersey is a neat feat if you can do it: marlin swim in the warm waters off the Florida coast. Point Pleasant is both a sports and commercial fishing center.

Point Pleasant Beach, N. J.

White Marlin

340

Clark's Landing is now a marina and restaurant. But sunsets on the Manasquan River are still spectacular. This is also the northern entry for the Intracoastal Waterway.

Point Pleasant, N.J. Grove and Pavilion, Clarks Landing.

341
Surf casting for bluefish.

342
Sunday Afternoon Bathers
by folk artist Dick LaBonte depicts
the beach at Bay Head in 1900
when there was a bathing pavillion
at the end of Bridge Avenue.

343

Philadelphia department store
owner John Wanamaker once had
a summer camp for his employees
on this island on the north side
of the Toms River.

344

The sneak box was originally
designed for use as a duck blind.
Small, with a shallow draft, this
broad-beamed sailing boat was
intended to be easily poled into
the reeds and camouflaged. It first
appeared in the 1830s. The design
was so popular that it was adapted
and produced in a variety of sizes
for different uses.

SNEAK BOX RACE.   ISLAND HEIGHTS, N. J.

345
Patrons stand in front of the
original carousel in Seaside Heights.

346
The Yum Yum Palace at
Great Adventure, one of the
three restaurants at the theme park
when it opened in 1973 in Jackson.

347

The once modest scope of
the Seaside Heights boardwalk.
The residential Seaside Park is
located farther south.

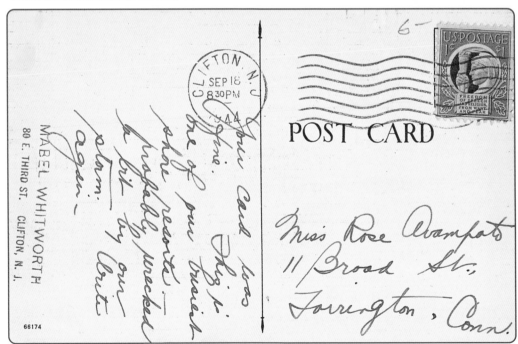

Aerial View Seaside Heights, and Seaside Park, N. J.

Photo by Maten

POST CARD

MABEL WHITWORTH
80 E. THIRD ST.
CLIFTON, N. J.

Miss Rose Avampato
11 Broad St.,
Torrington, Conn.

66174

Aerial View of Barnegat Light, N. J.

FEEDING SILK WORMS AT JOHN CHARLIE'S, BARNEGAT, N. J.

348
Barnegat State Park, the state's smallest park at thirty-six acres,
surrounds this lighthouse designed by George Gordon Meade
before he went on to military fame in the Civil War.
"Old Barney" anchors the treacherous shoals between
the northern tip of Long Beach Island and the southern tip
of Island Beach State Park.

349
In the early 1900s shoemaker John Charlie
briefly tried his hand at cultivating silkworms
as he had done in his native Syria. Mulberry
bushes still grow on the property, though his
house on Route 9 has been replaced by a bank.

350

The relic of a twenty-foot pound boat once deployed off Long Beach Island when the V-shaped pound nets were used to funnel schools of menhaden and cod into wooden boxes.

351

One of the Shore Region's other cash crops. By the middle of the twentieth century New Jersey was harvesting ten million pounds of cranberries a year.

PLANT No. 3 OF CRANBERRY CANNERS, INC. — NEW EGYPT, NEW JERSEY

Beautiful in Winter

as in Summer

AMERICA'S KESWICK

Keswick Grove, N.J.

352
Part center for alcoholic
rehabilitation, part Christian
missionary retreat, Keswick Colony
of Mercy was started in 1897
in Manchester Township by
William Raws of England.

THE HINDENBURG
Lakehurst, N. J.   1936

353
The most infamous of all zeppelins,
which cruised at ninety miles
an hour one thousand to three
thousand feet aboveground,
the luxury German dirigible
Hindenburg was commissioned
in 1936. On Thursday, May 6, 1937,
as it tried to dock at the Lakehurst
Naval Air Station, it exploded in a
ball of hydrogen-fueled fire.

A Close Game, Lakewood, N. J.

354
St. Alexander Nevsky Russian Orthodox Church
ministers to the community of Russian émigrés
who began arriving in Lakewood in the years
following World War II.

355
The game of kings on the George Jay Gould Estate,
which is now the home of Georgian Court College,
founded by the Sisters of Mercy in 1908.

The Delights of DELTIOLOGY

One day while vacationing on the isle of Mykonos, a resident of Athens sat down, scratched a few words into a small tablet, and then threw the loose page into the nearest mailbox, thus sending the first postcard.

Ok, so it really didn't happen that way in ancient Greece.

But the term for the study of postcards is called *deltiology* (del-tee-ology) from the Greek word *deltos* for writing tablets. Like stamps, postcards are easy to collect, don't take up a lot of space, and, for the beginner, are comparatively cheap as some cards go for just pennies. For the passionate deltiologist, however, the prices can become stratospheric—at auction a single, rare postcard may fetch four figures.

As with all hobbies, the interest in postcard collecting starts out innocently enough. It usually begins with your hometown. Familiar landmarks follow, such as the school you attended, the corner store, your house of worship. Then you branch out, looking for places you visited as a child, maybe where you went on your first date or the commemoration of a historical event that has meaning to your family. By this point, your preferences start to emerge. You may decide to focus on a single city, perhaps on a region or then again on a topic such as amusement parks, railroad stations, farm scenes, architecture, or African Americans. You may even develop an appreciation for the more technical aspects of postcard production, such as black-and-white photo cards, the more modern glossy chromes, or the textured linens.

Collections are enhanced with complementary postcards loosely referred to as "go-withs," such as interior and exterior building views. Some devotees create shadow boxes using postcards to go with ticket stubs, trinkets, programs, and other assorted memorabilia to put together a story of an event or location. Serious postcard collectors maintain checklists of the cards they have and of the cards they want or need to complete a collection. A checklist of the postcards used in this book follows after this chapter.

Because of the state's unique crossroads location in history, travel, commerce, ethnic demographics, and pop culture, New Jersey postcards are sought after by collectors living within and outside its borders. The more the Garden State is reshaped by current events, the more its rural and urban postcards are sought after for their nostalgic and historical value. Invariably, all collectors have scenes that no longer exist, and over time, as these collections are supplemented, they become the most prized.

Historians and civic planners use postcards as reference tools for studying vanished neighborhoods, landscapes, and even professions. Sometimes they are used as evidence in public hearings. Often the messages are part of the documentation that supports research into social trends.

NEW JERSEY is home to several significant postcard collections. Postcards reflecting the history of medicine, with a special focus on the health science history in New Jersey, are housed at the George F. Smith Library at the University of Medicine and Dentistry of New Jersey in Newark. The Local History and Genealogy Department at the Joint Free Public Library of Morristown and Morris Township has a Jerseyana postcard collection with an emphasis on Morristown, Morris Township, and Morris County. Both the Atlantic City and the Asbury Park libraries have resort collections of their respective seaside cities.

The Special Collections and University Archives at the Alexander Library of Rutgers University in New Brunswick and the New Jersey Department of the State Library in Trenton each have collections of postcards of towns throughout the state. The Trenton Public Library has a postcard collection of the capital city. The Camden and Atlantic County historical societies have collections, as do many individual historical societies, large and small, such as that of Wildwood and Lake Hopatcong in Landing. Appointments are required to view some of these collections, so it's a good idea to call ahead.

New Jersey views no longer in commercial circulation are also represented in out-of-state repositories. Those published by the Tichnor Brothers of Boston are part of the Tichnor Collection in the Print Department of the Boston Public Library. The Curt Teich Postcard Archives, the nation's largest public collection of advertising and view postcards and related materials, is located at the Lake County Forest Preserves, a museum and educational facility in Wauconda, Illinois, a northern suburb of Chicago.

The most recent history and 19,307-postcard checklist of the Detroit Publishing Company was published in 1994 by Nancy Stickels Stechschult, 1 Kingston Cove, Hilton Head, SC 29928. She printed a separate addition and corrections to the checklist in 1997. The company existed from 1895 to 1936.

BASIC POSTCARD categories are intertwined with early postal history and are generally recognized as follows:

Postal mailing cards. In 1873 Congress authorized the U.S. Post Office to produce single-sided mailing cards partly in response to the growing number of postcards imported from Germany, where lithographic reproduction on stone had reached a sophisticated and commercially appealing level. Eventually zinc plates on which the images were etched would replace the stones. Up to this point, public mail in America was confined to sealed letters of private correspondence for a fixed price of two cents. The new U.S. postal cards sold for one cent each.

Private pictorial postcards. In May 1893 black-and-white halftone postcards were printed to promote the World's Columbian Exhibition in Chicago. Postcards published between 1893 and 1898 are referred to as pioneer cards.

Private mailing cards. On May 19, 1898, Congress allowed private enterprises to publish and sell postcards, putting them in direct competition with those printed by the U.S. Post Office. The back, or verso, side was printed with the words "private mailing card" or "souvenir postcards" to make the distinction for the consumer. The front usually depicted a local view. Simple salutations were restricted to the front; the undivided back was reserved solely for names and addresses.

Colored cards. In 1899 the Detroit Publishing Company printed the first colored image postcard in the United States by acquiring the exclusive rights to a German process in which the four primary colors were applied separately during the printing process. The result gave a painterly quality to the photograph. A related process to which pink-colored ink was added, thus producing brown or sepia tones, was most notably used by the Albertype Company of Brooklyn. The word *albertype* is commonly applied to all brown-colored prints. Avidly printed until about 1920, both types of postcards are popular purchases because of the nostalgia their colors evoke.

Post card. On December 24, 1901, Congress authorized the use of the words *post card* to be printed on the privately printed cards and thus launched the glory days of postcard sending and collecting. Although the craze peaked about 1908, the era lasted until 1915, with senders squeezing their messages across the images on the front of the cards or in the tiny white borders some publishers provided at the bottom of the cards.

Divided backs. On March 1, 1907, Congress allowed for the verso side to be divided up between the sender and the receiver, that is, equal space for the address and for the message. The result was the freeing up of the front of the cards for full-frame images that would not be crowded by handwriting. As a category, the divided-back era lasted until 1915.

White-bordered. Launched by five-and-dime king Frank W. Woolworth in 1912, cheaply produced white-bordered cards featured a slim white border on all four sides that acted as a frame around the view. Woolworth cards specifically are identified by a W within a triangle in the lower left corner of the message side, although the low-cost, high-volume strategy unleashed many knockoff competitors. This turn of events is generally credited with the decline in the quality of postcard production. At the same time, the increased use of photographs in popular magazines and newspapers diverted the public's attention away from the novelty of photographic images on postcards, further adding to the decline in postcard purchases. The white-bordered era lasted until 1930.

Linen. The high rag content of the paper used to produce linen cards resulted in a textured surface similar to the fabric. This era, from 1930 to 1939, was also significant for the use of bright, sometimes garish, colors. Not surprisingly, this format attracted the attention of businesses, which adopted the use of linen cards by the thousands in their direct-mail advertising campaigns. The linen era is also a favorite collectible category because many cards depict the American way of life before World War II.

Chrome. The photochrome era, from 1939 to the present, was begun by the Union Oil series of 1939 and coincided with advances in photography that ironically signaled the modern-day decline of sending postcards. The public could afford to buy inexpensive cameras with which to take souvenir photos of the family vacation. However, chrome postcards are a strong collectible category, particularly cards most commonly used to depict pop culture tourist sites. Until the last decade of the twentieth century, chrome postcards were comparatively inexpensive. But prices started to climb, especially as the amusement piers and parks frequented by the 1950s baby boom generation began to disappear.

Reproduction (or repro). Reproduction cards are based on old negatives or on a public or private collection. Often they are reasonably priced and are attractive to amateur historians, novice collectors, and souvenir seekers.

Rack card. Begun as a new collectibles category sometime around 1997, rack cards (free advertising cards) are standard-size postcards commonly found in supermarkets and used to promote the purchase of anything from hot dogs to fruit drinks.

Continental. Continentals comprise the "bigger is better" category. Beginning around the last decade of the twentieth century, postcards increased in size from three-and-a-half-by-five-inch to four-by-six-inch—the better to stand out on a rack or in the mail.

Silk and tinseling. Silks refer to the threads attached to cards, creating garments worn by the model image. Tinseling refers to the glitter that postcard retailers added to boost sluggish sales of black-and-white views.

Real photo card. Real photo cards are black-and-white photos and are at the top end of the collectibles market in terms of price. They depict everything from train and car wrecks, hurricane aftermaths, and fires to popular leisure scenes of the day. New Jersey has a number of photographers whose postcards are among the most collected. The dimness that overcomes some of these photo cards can sometimes be cleared up by using a chamois cloth and a very light application of buff-colored shoe polish that is gently rubbed across the image. This process rarely damages the image.

WHILE it might be tempting to exercise some civic pride and claim that every New Jersey postcard ever printed is a collectible, honesty dictates otherwise. Major categories that are relevant to New Jersey postcards are:

Locations and destinations—especially if the originals have been altered or eliminated.

Roadside America—New Jersey is the archetypal drive-by state, bisected by national roads, county highways, and Main Streets too numerous to count. Along the sides of these roads people stopped to rest, to sleep, to relax, to eat, to shop, and to amuse themselves. Railroad stations, trolleys, canals, and related topics of transportation are perennial favorites. Ditto military, fire companies, firehouses, lighthouses, and lifesaving stations, which were established first in New Jersey.

African American and Judaica cards—challenging topics to collect because of their rarity; few photographs of African Americans in New Jersey were ever taken and printed as postcards, and a relatively small number of temple postcards were printed in comparison to Christian churches. The cards of synagogues are all the more dear because so many of the original structures were built from wood and eventually lost to fire.

Advertising cards—from cartoonist Thomas Nast to art deco; automobile showrooms, movie theaters, clothing stores, restaurants, banks, drugstores (both interiors and exteriors). Includes artist-signed postcards, such as the series of bathing beauties done by Hamilton King and published by J. T. Wilcox in 1907.

Sports cards—especially baseball from the early twentieth century and postcards that feature players. Hard to find is Roosevelt Stadium in Jersey City, where the Port Liberte residential complex is located, Water Stadium in Perth Amboy, and Reppert Stadium in Newark.

ON-LINE AUCTIONS are popular venues for finding postcards. So are flea markets and antique stores and secondhand bookshops. But if you want to find historians, both hobbyists and professionals, who can help you identify your postcards, go to the ephemera shows sponsored by local postcard clubs and/or dealers or to the clubs' regular meetings.

The Garden State Postcard Club (GSPCC) is the oldest collectors' club in New Jersey and is the third oldest in the country after New York City's and Rhode Island's. Other clubs throughout the state are: Jersey Shore Postcard Club (Box 6533, Fair Haven, NJ 07704; same address for GSPCC); Central Jersey Deltiological Society (23 Plymouth Court, Piscataway, NJ 08854), the South Jersey Postcard Club (4 Plymouth Drive, Marlton, NJ 08053), and the Washington Crossing Postcard Club (Box 39, Washington Crossing, PA 18977; meetings held in Titusville, New Jersey).

Each year the International Federation of Postcard Dealers (Box 1765, Manassas, VA 20108) publishes a free guide of all its members. The *Postcard Collector* (Box 1050, Dubuque, IA 52004) is a monthly publication with features on ephemera, and *Barr's Post Card News* (70 South Sixth Street, Lansing, IA 52151) is a biweekly newspaper filled chiefly with lists of postcards for sale.

A ring binder and acid-free plastic sleeves are all it takes to get you started. If you are weak on Garden State geography, write to the state Department of Transportation and ask for the book on place names: Communications Office, Box 600, Trenton, NJ 08625.

356
In February 1906 the young Marie signed this German-made
West Orange view card and sent it to Sheepshead Bay,
Long Island, New York.

357
New Jersey's oldest collectors' club
celebrated its twenty-fifth anniversary
with this card designed by member Don Preziosi,
a long-time deltiologist who writes the
"Linens & Beyond" column
for *The Postcard Collector.*

358
Captain John H. Young
was an entertainment mogul,
enthusiastically promoting all kinds
of acts, rides, and shams on his pier.
This early card made of heavy paper
stock lets the buyer know the card
was not printed by the government.

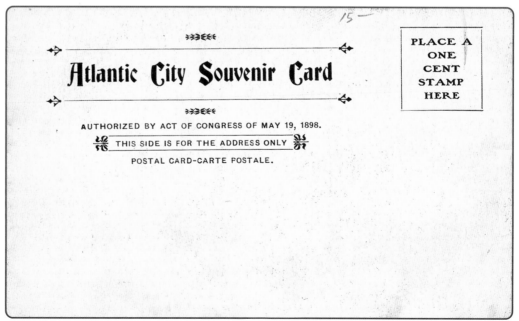

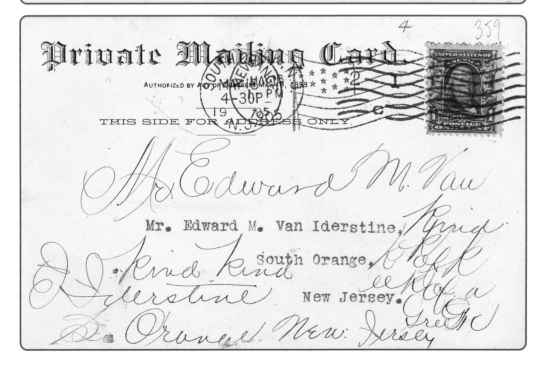

What kind of
a Greek Puzzle
do you think
that Postal Card
is?
   Very kind of
George to do all
that writing,
why did he not
address it also?

Pretty good
game, but I

saw how it was played. I'm not as thick as I look.

        ?RETTEL TAHT S'EREHW

                        NEMA.

359

The writer got the optimum use
of this leftover private mailing card
sent in 1905.

360

Black-and-white photographs were colored with vegetable dye after they were on card stock, as seen in this German-made postcard distributed by P. P. Sweeten of Pedricktown, now in Oldmans Township in Salem County.

Railroad Avenue, Pedricktown, N. J.

361

A white-bordered card.

PUSEY & JONES SHIPBUILDING CO. GLOUCESTER, N. J.

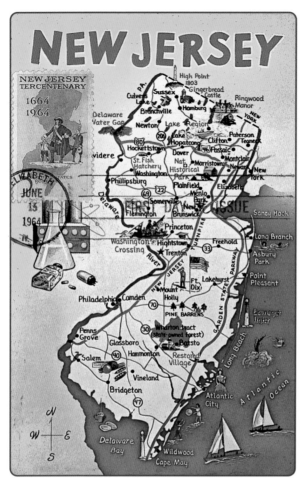
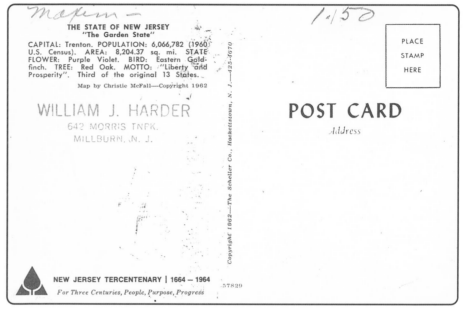

362

A modern example of a divided-back card is this one from the Scheller Company of Hackettstown
that was made in anticipation of New Jersey's three hundredth anniversary in 1964.
Mechanical engineer–turned–professional photographer George Scheller
started in the postcard business in 1951 with aerial views he shot
using a forty-pound Fairchild F 56 camera he hung out an airplane window.
His favorite four-by-five-inch format view camera is the Swiss-made Sinar.

363

Categorized as the "Bird's-Eye View Artist of Vacation Resorts" by the Half Moon Postcard Club, Wurtsboro, New York, Alfred S. Landis had New Jersey studios in Newark, Bayview, and Beachwood. With pen and brush Landis stylized views, often making them more grandiose than they were to satisfy the promotional needs of his hotel clients.

SEIDLER'S BEACH, LAWRENCE HARBOR, N. J. SHORE ROUTE NO. 35. P. O. CLIFFWOOD, N. J. PHONE MATAWAN 208. FISH—SHORE—CHICKEN DINNERS.

364

Newark photographer William H. Broadwell knew the value of self-promotion.

WM. H. BROADWELL, COMMERCIAL PHOTOGRAPHER, AT HIGH POINT PARK. SUSSEX CO., N. J.

LAKE HOPATCONG
WE ARE LOOKING FOR A MAN
ANY OLD MAN WILL DO
COPYRIGHT-06
W.J. HARRIS

BAPTISMAL SERVICE AT CANTON BAPTIST CHURCH,
PHOTOGRAPH BY WM. J. S. BRADWAY, HANCOCK'S BRIDGE, N.J.

365
William J. Harris was the most
prolific photographer around
Lake Hopatcong, known as much
for his postcard views as for the
captions on his photo cards.
He also had studios in Pennsylvania
and Florida.

366
The black-and-white photo cards
of South Jersey photographer
William Bradway are highly
prized among collectors for their
photographic and documentation
values.

367
The Hightstown Railroad Station, photographed by the Thorburn Studio.

368
William B. Cooper of Medford photographed a lot of local scenes, including this one when the post office opened in Camden in 1899.

Opera House, Cranford, N.J.

OPERA HOUSE BLOCK FIRE
CRANFORD, N.J.

369 & 370
Before and After:
The Cranford Opera House
on a day when the roads are
being surveyed, printed in
Germany, and in the immediate
aftermath of a fire that destroyed
the block on February 3, 1912.

371 & 372

The go-withs: only the clock remains of the Colgate-Palmolive Company after the 141-year-old factory was closed in 1985. The company used a one-cent U.S. postal card for mailing coupons to customers.

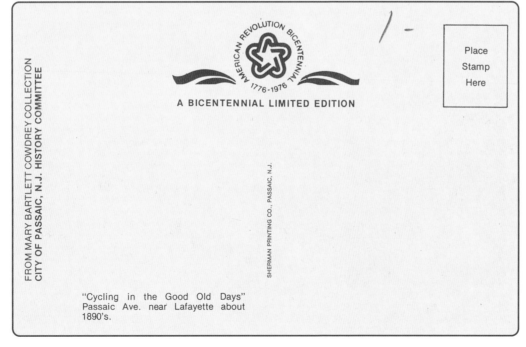

"Cycling in the Good Old Days"
Passaic Ave. near Lafayette about
1890's.

FROM MARY BARTLETT COWDREY COLLECTION
CITY OF PASSAIC, N.J. HISTORY COMMITTEE

AMERICAN REVOLUTION BICENTENNIAL
1776-1976

A BICENTENNIAL LIMITED EDITION

SHERMAN PRINTING CO., PASSAIC, N.J.

Place
Stamp
Here

373
This photograph was reproduced
as a special occasion postcard.

374

This is a linen of the Weequahic Diner at Elizabeth and Hawthorne Avenues, Newark, that was published by Benjamin H. Silverman, Newark.

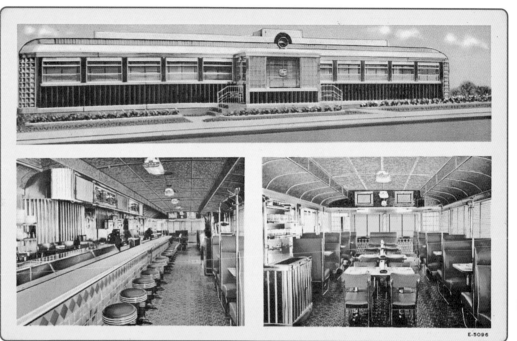

375

Roadside: early view of the Circus Drive-In on Route 35 in Wall Township.

ATLANTIC CITY
GIRL

H·King

COPYRIGHT, 1907, BY J.T. WILCOX.

376

Using charcoal, Hamilton King did a set
of twelve bathing beauty postcards that include
three from New Jersey. The other two
are Asbury Park and Ocean Grove.

Reward a PROGRESSIVE
School Board Man

He is
Both
a
Doctor
and
a
Lawyer

He
Stands
for a
Better
Hospital;

More
School
Facilities

527

Vote for Dr. Lovell

1. He voted for your new Union, Myrtle, Berkeley and Grove Schools.
2. A vote for him means a vote for a better hospital.
3. He makes no rash promises but will labor for better water and transportation.
4. A vote for him is a vote for intelligence in Irvington's government.

Elect Dr. Lovell Tuesday

Paid for by Wm. Rigney, Campaign Mgr.

 27

377

A political postcard—the older the better
because they tell more about the candidate
and the local community. School board member
John F. Lovell later ran for town commission
in 1930, and won again.

Marching through Jersey

We were not troubled by these "soldiers."

"E. S."

378
Franz Huld of New York produced a number
of different humorous mosquito postcards,
several for the New Jersey market.

379
Continentals, large, four-by-six-inch postcards,
are the newcomers in collectibles.
Ocean Grove photographer Frank Saragnese
donated this image to the Save Tillie Campaign
as a fund-raiser to preserve the funny face
on the Palace Amusements building in Asbury Park.

Postcard Checklist

NO.	TITLE	PUBLISHER & NUMBER	DATE
1	Greetings from New Jersey	Curteich, Chicago, #1B-H2219	
2	I Am Writing for a Living	J. Tully, Chicago	c. 1907
3	$5.00 Reward	American Novelty Co., Atlantic City, N.J., #127	c. 1905
4	Greetings from Asbury Park	Plastichrome, Boston, #AP-50	c. 1970
5	A Typical Boardwalk Scene	P.C.D. Co., #R-24790	c. 1912
6	The Kids from Morristown, N.J.	United Art Pub. Co., New York, #1405	c. 1909
7	Brook's Store, Washington St.	E. Brooks, Hoboken, N.J., #1	c. 1905
8	Brook's Store, Headquarters	E. Brooks, Hoboken, N.J., #2	c. 1905
9	Dedication of "The Billy Sunday Tabernacle"	Albertype Co., Brooklyn, N.Y.	1915
10	Lotus Lilies	E. W. Humphreys, Woodstown, N.J., #50875	c. 1900
11	On of L.V.R.R. The Old Farmhouse at Bellewood	Hugh C. Leighton Co., Portland, Maine, #6118	c. 1905
12	Tomb of Walt Whitman	Central News Co., Philadelphia, #11496	c. 1906
13	The *Jersey Central Flyer*	H. C. Leighton Co., Portland, Maine, #951	c. 1906
14	Ferry Boat	M. L. Metrochrome	c. 1915
15	John Bull Monument	Art Photo Greeting Co., New York	c. 1891
16	Flying High in Atlantic City	Frank B. Hubin's Big Post Card Store, Atlantic City, N.J.	1907
17	New Dreamland Arena	Harry H. Baumann, New York, #6441	c. 1940
18	S.S. *Morro Castle,* Asbury Park	Stickler Photo, Asbury Park, N.J.	c. 1935
19	Passaic River Bridge	Tichnor, Boston, #84303	c. 1951

NO.	TITLE	PUBLISHER & NUMBER	DATE
20	Garden State Parkway	Tichnor, Boston, #84305	c. 1952
21	China Land Restaurant	Tichnor, Boston, #79242	c. 1950
22	New Post Office Building	Colourpicture, Boston, #11343	c. 1947
23	Wise Guys of Newark, N.J.	#578-1	c. 1911
24	State of New Jersey	Mayrose Co., New York	c. 1940
25	Clipper Passing Statue of Liberty	A. Mainzer, New York, #80	c. 1931
26	Tice Tavern	A Mainzer, New York, #2132	c. 1911
27	Pennsylvania Railroad Depot	American News Co., New York, #6811	c. 1907
28	Entrance to Lincoln Park	Tichnor, Boston, #64980	c. 1930
29	There Is No Speed Limit		c. 1910
30	Journal Square	Interborough News Co., New York, #8A-H289	c. 1940
31	Castle Point	J. Koehler, #15	c. 1905
32	Fire Boat	F. G. Temme Co., Orange, N.J., #89T	c. 1905
33	The Hamburg-American Line	#96-52	c. 1910
34	Hudson River Tunnel	#96-48	c. 1908
35	Clam Broth House	Color Promotions, New York, #165262	c. 1970
36	Karl Bitter's Studio	John C. Voigt, Jersey City, N.J., #49	c. 1900
37	Hamilton Monument		c. 1920
38	Lincoln Tunnel	Pendor Natural Color, Pearl River, N.Y., #24044-B	c. 1970
39	The Twin State and Capitol Theatre	Manhattan Post Card Co., New York, #17056	c. 1930
40	Capt. Baldwin Making His First Flight		c. 1909
41	Palisades and Hudson River	Albertype Co., Brooklyn, N.Y.	c. 1938
42	George Washington Bridge	Mayrose Co., Linden, N.J.	1948
43	Palisades Amusement Park	Pendor Natural Color, Pearl River, N.Y., #17491	c. 1960
44	Bridge, Showing Post Office	W. S. Brown, River Edge, N.J., #1454	c. 1905
45	Arcola Mill	B. Dropkin, Ridgewood, N.J.	c. 1934
46	Brown's Grand View Lodge	Dexter Press, Pearl River, N.Y., #21139	c. 1930
47	Bobbink and Atkins Nurserymen	Garraway Photo Art, Rutherford, N.J., #51	c. 1908
48	The Meadowlands	Scheller Co., Hackettstown, N.J., #151171	c. 1977
49	Greenwood Lake	Dexter Press/Pendor, Pearl River, N.Y., #20154-B	c. 1960
50	Factories along Passaic River	#252-1023	c. 1909
51	John P. Holland Monument	Ruben Publishing, Newburgh, N.Y., #4A-H528	c. 1939
52	Patterson Silk Exposition	Albertype Co., Brooklyn, N.Y.	1914
53	Belle Vista Castle	#63282	c. 1911
54	Passaic Falls in Winter	#83289	c. 1911
55	Greetings from Newark	#63536	c. 1912

Postcard
Checklist

232

NO.	TITLE	PUBLISHER & NUMBER	DATE
56	New Park Place Station	N.J. Post Card Co., Newark, N.J., #P-63540	c. 1911
57	Robert Treat Hotel	Sackett & Wilhelms Corp., New York, #30780	c. 1916
58	Market Street from Broad Street		c. 1909
59	A Row of the Finest on Parade	#1308	c. 1905
60	Friedman's Music Shop	Curt Teich, Chicago, #2A552	c. 1940
61	Mosque Theatre	Emil Frankl, Newark, N.J., #20382, No. 291	c. 1930
62	End of the Heat	Temme Co., #101	c. 1905
63	Newark Theatre		c. 1910
64	Julian Eltinge	I. Stern, New York	c. 1905
65	Ballantine's Gate-way	#1319	c. 1905
66	Bird's-eye View	#63497	c. 1912
67	The Sand Court	F. G. Temme, Orange, N.J., #3749	c. 1908
68	Greetings from Montclair	F. G. Temme, Orange, N.J., #371	c. 1910
69	Newark Airport	Tichnor, Boston, #62191	c. 1935
70	Who'll Bring Home the Bacon	Prudential Insurance Co., Newark, N.J.	c. 1940
71	Hair Styles—1970	I. E. Walker, Passaic, N.J., #81961	1970
72	New Pennsylvania R.R. Station	Ruben Publishing Co., Newburgh, N.Y., #5A-H841	c. 1935
73	Birthplace of Ex-President Cleveland	#V-285	c. 1907
74	Crystal Lake Amusement Park	Landis & Alsop, Newark, N.J., #28748	c. 1920
75	Orange Centennial 1807–1907		1907
76	South Mountain Arena	Lewis Studios, Orange, N.J., #S-55655	c. 1950
77	Office of Thos. A. Edison	#2425	c. 1905
78	Rahway River	#4346	c. 1920
79	B. Altman & Co.		1957
80	Paper Mill Playhouse	Albertype Co., Brooklyn, N.Y.	c. 1950
81	Castles Ice Cream	Parker-Brawner Co., Washington, D.C., #61439	c. 1915
82	Water Front from Staten Island	Souvenir Post Card Co., New York, #23281	c. 1900
83	Old Ladies Home	Line & Co., Elizabeth, N.J., #62	c. 1930
84	Company No. 3, Elizabeth, N.J.	Elizabeth Novelty Co., Elizabeth, N.J.	c. 1906
85	New Journal Building	Photo & Art Postal Card Co., New York, #27316	c. 1915
86	Greater Mt. Teman Church	Dexter Press, West Nyack, N.Y., #34389-C	c. 1965
87	The Story of Reverend Caldwell	Dexter Press, Pearl River, N.Y./ Nathan Weinstein, Union, N.J., #27728	c. 1940
88	Baltursol Golf Club	New Jersey Post Card Co., Newark, N.J., #A-67805	c. 1920
89	Union, N.J.	Pendor, Pearl River, N.Y., #33363-C	c. 1950
90	Wheatenaville	Wheatena Co., Rahway, N.J.	c. 1932
91	Dining Room	Valentine & Sons, New York, #200591	c. 1908

NO.	TITLE	PUBLISHER & NUMBER	DATE
92	Ye Olde Historical Inn	New Jersey Publishing Co., Newark, N.J., #A-62949	c. 1920
93	Esso Research Center		c. 1949
94	Candy Pavilion		c. 1908
95	Raritan Yacht Club	Souvenir Post Card Co., New York, #23342	c. 1905
96	Smith Street	Leighton & Valentine Co., New York	c. 1912
97	The Synagogue of Congregation Sharey Tfillah		c. 1906
98	The Edison Tower	Thomas Alvin Edison Foundation	c. 1937
99	Henry Ford and Thomas Edison	Artcraft Photo Co., Rutherford, N.J.	c. 1925
100	The Walker-Gordon Rotolactor	Art Photo Greeting Co., Elizabeth, N.J.	c. 1950
101	This Is the Kind We Grow	#148	c. 1916
102	Johnson & Johnson's Factory	#1074	c. 1910
103	Bird's-eye View	Curteich, Chicago, #9A-H555	c. 1940
104	George Street, New Brunswick, N.J.	Temme Co., Orange, N.J., #2204	c. 1910
105	Gateway to Rutgers College	Temme Co., Orange, N.J., #2167	c. 1910
106	Camp Kilmer		c. 1949
107	World War Memorial Monument	Curteich, Chicago, #8A-H2707	c. 1930
108	High Point Park, N.J.	W. H. Broadwell, Newark, N.J.	c. 1930
109	Main Street, Sussex, N.J.	E. Fisher, Sussex, N.J.	c. 1905
110	Playboy Great Gorge		c. 1970
111	Rifle Range, Camp Wawayanda	Artvue Post Card Co., New York	c. 1919
112	Castle Edward	Temme Co., Newark, N.J., #2355	c. 1915
113	River Styx Bridge	#3921	c. 1905
114	Alamac Hotel	W. J. Harris, Lake Hopatcong, N.J., #103755	c. 1914
115	Unique Gingerbread Castle	Tichnor, Boston, #77301	c. 1930
116	Humpty Dumpty	American Aerial Survey, Hackettstown, N.J., #28163	c. 1940
117	Swartswood, N.J.	Albertype Co., Brooklyn, N.Y.	c. 1915
118	Green Pond, N.J.	Photograph Co., New York, #65789	c. 1909
119	Manitou Island	Curteich, Chicago, #OC155-N	c. 1951
120	The Pavilion, Cranberry Lake, N.J.	F. G. Temme Co., Orange, N.J.	c. 1915
121	Delaware Water Gap	Pocono Scenicards & Photographics, Stroudsburg, Pa., #42736-B	c. 1950
122	Myers Ferry	G. V. Millar & Co., Scranton, Pa., #8820	c. 1905
123	Land of Make Believe	Colourpicture, Boston	c. 1955
124	Hot Dog Johnny	Dexter Press/Pocono Scenicards, East Stroudsburg, Pa., #63554-B	c. 1950
125	Junction of the Lehigh and Delaware Rivers	Leo Meyer, Easton, Pa., #R-70980	c. 1905
126	View on Morris Canal	F. W. Kluppelberg's Son, Hackettstown, N.J., #50479	c. 1905

NO.	TITLE	PUBLISHER & NUMBER	DATE
127	Main Street, Hackettstown, N.J.	F. W. Kluppelberg's Son, Hackettstown, N.J., #50488	c. 1909
128	Musconetcong Trout Stream	Ruben Publishing Co., Newburgh, N.Y., #1A2867	c. 1920
129	Girl's Parlor C.C. I.	F. W. Kluppelberg's Son, Hackettstown, N.J., #64752	c. 1910
130	Dorset Breeding-Ewes	F. W. Kluppelberg's Son, Hackettstown, N.J., #52062	c. 1905
131	Budd's Beach	Norton's, Budd Lake, N.J., #77738	c. 1940
132	Municipal Building and Beach	Norton's, Budd Lake, N.J., #77733	c. 1940
133	Wild West City	Dexter Press, West Nyack, N.Y., #DR-29214-B	c. 1960
134	St. Francis Health Resort	Albertype Co., Brooklyn, N.Y.	c. 1915
135	The Home of Tempe Wick	Tichnor, Boston, #62062	c. 1940
136	Washington's Headquarters	Rotograph Co., New York, #2092	c. 1907
137	Home of the Morse Telegraph		c. 1905
138	Municipal Building	Washington News Depot, Morristown, N.J., #132975	c. 1932
139	Headquarters of Seeing Eye	Tichnor, Boston, #80901	c. 1940s
140	Brook Lake Chime Tower	#3965	c. 1920
141	Asbury Hall	F. G. Temme, Orange, N.J., #E385	c. 1906
142	Bottle Hill Restaurant	D. E. Hillthal, Rutherford, N.J., #36664-B	c. 1950
143	Ryland Inn	Chester Printing Service, Newark, N.J.	c. 1940
144	F. C. Williams Produce Market		c. 1940
145	Far Hills Inn	Morris Advertising Service, Somerville, N.J., #S-58205	c. 1950
146	Canal View	J. W. Moore, Bound Brook, N.J., #1596	c. 1905
147	Pathé Frères Moving Pictures	Fetterly & Loree, Druggists, Bound Brook, N.J., #314	c. 1905
148	Fire Houses	Fetterly & Loree, Pharmacists, Bound Brook, N.J., #3729	c. 1905
149	Ensemble Broadcast		c. 1915
150	Belle Mead Farm	E. C. Kropp Co., Milwaukee, #12571	c. 1910
151	State of New Jersey	S. Langsdorf & Co., New York	c. 1915
152	Duke's Park	Harry A. Bird, Somerville, N.J., #2954	c. 1915
153	The Conservatory	Valentine & Sons, New York, #202404	c. 1915
154	The Brownie Band	Valentine & Sons, New York, #202402	c. 1915
155	Wallace House	A. C. Bosselman & Co., New York, #2092	c. 1910
156	Green Sergeant's Bridge	Scheller Co., Hackettstown, N.J., #20752	c. 1950
157	Stanton Mill		c. 1907
158	Circle Diner	M. Clavolino, Clinton, N.J., #25456-B	c. 1955
159	Union Hotel, Flemington, N.J.	Mayrose Co., New York	c. 1925
160	Flemington Athletic Field	E. Vosseller, Flemington, N.J., #5104	c. 1915
161	From the Studio of Mary Sunderlin	Mary Sunderlin, Flemington, N.J.	c. 1908
162	Union Street Looking South	Local View Ptg. Co., New York	c. 1915

163	Shad Fishing	J. B. Kline & Son, Lambertville, N.J.	c. 1915
164	St. John Terrell's Music Circus	Joseph F. Morsello, Philadelphia, #56892	c. 1940
165	Roeblings Wire Mills	Valentine & Sons, New York, #200399	c. 1909
166	A View of Some of the Potteries	#63822	c. 1905
167	Balloon Ascension	A. L. Opdyke, Trenton, N.J., #100792	c. 1905
168	Fruit and Vegetable Exhibit	A. L. Opdyke, Trenton, N.J., #100798	c. 1905
169	State House from River	#97-18	c. 1910
170	Legislative Chamber	F. G. Temme, Orange, N.J., #179	c. 1912
171	Trenton Makes—The World Takes	Scheller Co., Hackettstown, N.J., #121001	1970
172	New Jersey State Barracks	#29117	c. 1920
173	State Street Lock	#63800	c. 1910
174	McConkey Homestead	#63831	c. 1912
175	Steamer *Burlington*	E. M. Watson, Trenton, N.J.	c. 1908
176	The Falls, Hightstown, N.J.	Eagle Post Card View Co., New York	c. 1940
177	Railroad Hotel	Leighton & Valentine Co., New York, #207290	c. 1915
178	Peddie Institute, Hightstown, N.J.	Thorburn Studio, Hightstown, N.J.	c. 1905
179	Rah! Rah! Rah! Rah!		c. 1920
180	Nassau Hall	Curt Teich & Co., Chicago, #4A-H1366	c. 1920
181	Nassau Inn, Princeton, N.J.	Christine Whiteman, Princeton, N.J.	c. 1920
182	Blair Hall and Station	Illustrated Postal Card Co., New York	c. 1915
183	The Old Bonaparte Park House	Will H. Carslake, Druggist, Bordentown, N.J.	c. 1910
184	School House	Geo F. Deacon, Bordentown, N.J., #2145	c. 1905
185	River Bank, Beverly, N.J.	H. T. Simon, Beverly, N.J., #D2316	c. 1909
186	Shore Club Houses	Fasler & Kirchener	c. 1905
187	Riverfront at Billingsport, N.J.	E. W. Humphreys, Woodstown, N.J., #181	c. 1905
188	Ulrica at Pier Penn's Grove	E. W. Humphreys, Woodstown, N.J., #224	c. 1905
189	Public Library, Burlington, N.J.	Commercial Printing Co., Burlington, N.J.	c. 1908
190	Home of J. Fenimore Cooper	American News Co., New York, #13745	c. 1908
191	Camp Dix, N.J.		c. 1945
192	Life at Camp Dix, N.J.	Underwood & Underwood, New York	c. 1917
193	Log Cabin Lodge	Curteich, Chicago, #9B-H715	c. 1930
194	The Canoe Club	Albertype Co., Brooklyn, N.Y.	c. 1930
195	Turnpike Motel	Curteich, Chicago, #2C-H929	c. 1950
196	Batsto Stage	Jack Freeman, Inc., Longport, N.J., #100854	c. 1970
197	Historic Whitesbog	Whitesbog Preservation Trust	c. 1920
198	Your Friends in Lawnside	#2103	c. 1910
199	Greetings from Camden	Curteich, Chicago, #3B-H645	c. 1947
200	Home of Victor Talking Machine	Illustrated Postal Card Co., New York, #205	c. 1908

NO.	TITLE	PUBLISHER & NUMBER	DATE
201	Peerless Pearl Co.		c. 1940
202	Linden Street, Camden, N.J.	Standard Post Card Co., Philadelphia	c. 1915
203	Walt Whitman Hotel	Mayrose Co., Linden, N.J.	c. 1920
204	Campbell's Kids	#1	c. 1909
205	Boat Races on Cooper River	#48601	c. 1920
206	Colonial House	Flitcraft & Fowler, Haddonfield, N.J., #2121	c. 1905
207	On the Mall at Cherry Hill	WYCO Products, Jenkintown, Pa., #85-G	1961
208	Garden State Park		c. 1985
209	Hill Theatre	Mayrose Co., Linden, N.J.	c. 1930
210	Summit Park in the Grove	S. P. Clark, Pitman, N.J., #439	c. 1907
211	Lake Narraticon	Guest & Guest, Swedesboro, N.J., #1164	c. 1908
212	Esso	Collotype Co., Elizabeth, N.J.	c. 1940
213	Roller Coaster, Riverview Beach	Alvis W. Wallace, Pennsville, N.J., #92741	c. 1925
214	Range Finder, Fort Mott, N.J.	W. H. Andrews & Co., Druggists, Salem, N.J., #D2470	c. 1910
215	Broadway, Salem, N.J.	E. W. Humphreys, Woodstown, N.J.	c. 1907
216	A Country "Vendue"	E. W. Humphreys, Woodstown, N.J.	c. 1905
217	Hancock House	Curt Teich, Chicago, #4A-H2192	c. 1920
218	A Busy Day at the Potato Market	H. S. Foster, Elmer, N.J.	c. 1905
219	Sunset at Salem Creek	Wm. H. Andrews & Co., Salem, N.J., #2405	c. 1905
220	Welcome to Cape May	Curteich, Chicago	c. 1964
221	S.S. *New Jersey*	East Farthing, Rehoboth Beach, Del., #S-58516-1	c. 1964
222	Pink House	Curteich, Chicago, #103	c. 1964
223	Light House by Moonlight	Tichnor, Boston, #60735	c. 1949
224	Concrete Ship *Atlantus*	Tichnor, Boston, #62960	c. 1930
225	Horseshoe Crab	Dexter Press/Sandpiper Photos, Fortescue, N.J., #84773-D	c. 1960
226	Cape May Avenue, Whitesboro, N.J.		c. 1910
227	East Point Lighthouse	Sandpiper Photos, Fortescue, N.J., #34690-E	c. 1960
228	Unloading Oysters	F. M. Kirby & Co., #A-4666	c. 1905
229	An Afternoon's Catch	Albertype Co., Brooklyn, N.Y.	c. 1910
230	Ledge Lighthouse, Delaware Bay	H. S. Foster, Elmer, N.J.	c. 1906
231	Palace of Depression	Tichnor, Boston, #78302	c. 1930
232	J. A. Washburne		1911
233	Vineland Grape Juice	C. H. Graves	c. 1905
234	Chicken Farm, Vineland, N.J.	Lynn H. Boyer, Philadelphia, #62372	c. 1920
235	Little Robin Duck Farm		c. 1911
236	West Jersey and Jersey Southern R.R. Stations	Rotograph Co., New York, #A6391	c. 1905

NO.	TITLE	PUBLISHER & NUMBER	DATE
237	Wheaton Museum of Glass	Plastichrome, Boston, #P31083	c. 1980
238	Arial View of Seabrook Farms	Curteich, Chicago, #0C-H1729	c. 1950
239	Tomato Wagons	F. M. Kirby & Co., #50-3	c. 1905
240	National Vegetable Queen	Dexter Press/Connelly-Moy, Bridgeton, N.J., #79148	
241	Along the Bank	Pine & Whitaker, Bridgeton, N.Y., #G12495	c. 1905
242	The House Where the Tea Was Stored		c. 1905
243	Greenwich, N.J. Sep. 30-08		c. 1908
244	This Beats Joy Riding	Midland Publishing, New York, #86-4	c. 1913
245	4th of July Celebration	Geo. E. Mousley, Philadelphia, #7849	c. 1912
246	Entrance to Wildwood Crest, N.J.	Geo. E. Mousley, Philadelphia, #A-7872	c. 1905
247	Surfside Restaurant	Dexter Press/Douglas Hunsberger Photography, #59457-D	c. 1970
248	Casino, Wildwood, N.J.	American News Co., New York, #A12272	c. 1908
249	Sagel's Original Salt Water Taffy	R. W. Ryan, Wildwood, N.J., #57-60	c. 1905
250	Wildwood-by-the-Sea, N.J.		c. 1905
251	Sweet's Baths, Wildwood, N.J.	Smith Printing Co.	c. 1905
252	The Wildwoods by the Sea, N.J.	Cape May County Leader Co., Wildwood, N.J., #435	c. 1960
253	Holly Beach Life Saving Crew	Rotograph Co., New York, #53464	c. 1907
254	The "Hole Dam" Fish Family	Wildwood Post Card Co., Wildwood, N.J.	c. 1906
255	Hereford Light	R. W. Ryan, Wildwood, N.J., #11433	c. 1905
256	Stone Harbor, N.J.	Tichnor, Boston, #K-14644	c. 1970
257	Greetings from Sea Isle City	Colourpicture Publication, Boston, #K8347	c. 1940s
258	Beach and Bathing View	Colourpicture Publication, Boston, #K7842	c. 1954
259	Outdoor Swimming Pool	Tichnor, Boston, #135689	c. 1937
260	Greetings from Ocean City, N.J.	Colourpicture Publication, Boston, #P36149	c. 1950
261	Hubin's Big Post Card Store		c. 1910
262	Greetings from Atlantic City	Tichnor, Boston, #71	c. 1960
263	Automobile Routes to Atlantic City	American Bank Note, New York	c. 1910
264	Wharf at Longport		c. 1905
265	Miss America	Jack Freeman, Inc., Longport, N.J., #102524	c. 1970
266	The Cake Walkers	Osborne Pub. Co., Philadelphia	c. 1903
267	The World Famous Steel Pier	#15310N	c. 1940
268	Diving Horse	E. C. Kropp Co., Milwaukee, #31626	c. 1910
269	Steeple Chase Pier	E. C. Kropp Co., Milwaukee, #4971	c. 1950
270	Garden Pier, at Night	Post Card Distributing Co., Philadelphia	c. 1916
271	Greetings from Atlantic City	#17449N	c. 1940
272	Aeroplane Returning to Beach	Sithens Post Card Co., Atlantic City, N.J.	c. 1920

NO.	TITLE	PUBLISHER & NUMBER	DATE
273	Hotel Hygeia, Atlantic City	Gut & Steers, New York	c. 1916
274	Quaker City Express Buses	H. J. Cable, Haddon Heights, N.J., #76352	c. 1950
275	Allegheny Commuter	Laureate Press	c. 1970
276	Hygeia Baths	E. C. Kropp Co., Milwaukee	c. 1915
277	Sun & Star Roof	Edward Stern & Co., Inc., Philadelphia	c. 1950
278	Just Ran Across an Old Friend	Chilton Co., Philadelphia, #102	c. 1912
279	Heinz Pier		c. 1915
280	Planters Peanuts	E. C. Kropp Co., Milwaukee, #10475	c. 1940
281	Milton Latz Knife and Fork Inn		c. 1930
282	Getting Ready to Come Home	Chilton Printing Co., Philadelphia, #2539	c. 1915
283	Lobster King Harry Hackney	E. C. Kropp Co., Milwaukee, #19974	c. 1940
284	Mammy's Famous Shops	Lumitone Photoprint, New York	c. 1940
285	Help Yourself Help Atlantic City		1976
286	Be a Winner in Atlantic City	Jack Freeman, Inc., Longport, N.J.	1978
287	Dennis Farm Delicacies	Lumitone Photoprint, New York	c. 1942
288	Hotel Dennis Dining Room	Lumitone Photoprint, New York	c. 1940
289	The John Taylor Colonial Inn	Curteich, Chicago	c. 1955
290	The Elephant Hotel	P.C.D. Co., #R-24793	c. 1912
291	World Famous Dude Ranch	E. C. Kropp Co., Milwaukee, #25825	c. 1940
292	They're Off	Mayrose Co., Linden, N.J.	c. 1950
293	Greetings from the Army Airmen	Allied Printing, Atlantic City, N.J.	c. 1940
294	St. Nicholas Church	E. C. Kropp Co., Milwaukee, #20023	c. 1930
295	The Jersey Devil		1975
296	The Country General Store	KARDmasters, Allentown, Pa., #73757-B	c. 1950
297	Seaview Country Club	Curteich, Chicago, #9A-H971	c. 1948
298	E. Hornberger's Bakery	YorKolor Process, New York, #YL9517	c. 1960
299	Jimmie's & Larry's Hotel		c. 1920
300	Renault Vineyards	H. S. Crocker Co., San Bruno, Calif.	c. 1950
301	Dr. Smith's Sanitarium	H. Kirscht	c. 1914
302	Conner's Hotel	Aladdin Color, Florence, N.J., #135272	1973
303	Greetings from the Jersey Shore	Colourpicture, Boston, #P55923	c. 1960
304	Hendrick Hudson Springs	Tichnor, Boston, #138172	c. 1920
305	Lighthouse, Fort Hancock, N.J.		c. 1928
306	Projectile		c. 1907
307	Lighthouse, Highlands, N.J.		c. 1905
308	Aerial View of Peninsula House	Curteich, Chicago, #0B-H2132	
309	Ice Boat Racing	Curt Teich, Chicago, #57335	c. 1936
310	Broad Street, Red Bank, N.J.	Mayrose Co., New York	c. 1940

NO.	TITLE	PUBLISHER & NUMBER	DATE
311	Catawba–Concord	S. L. de Fabry, New York, #M-9074	c. 1912
312	Corner Store, Shrewsbury, N.J.	American News Co., New York, #A6723	c. 1909
313	Hanley-Page Bombing Machine	W. H. Bechtel, Asbury Park, N.J.	c. 1917
314	Monmouth Park Race Track	#86232	c. 1950
315	A Ramble through the Park	Arthur Livingston, New York, #566	c. 1906
316	What's Left of Merry-Go-Round	Acme Print, Asbury Park, N.J.	1944
317	Franklin Cottage	I. Stern, New York, #268	c. 1909
318	The Summer Capital		1916
319	Murray Guggenheim Cottage	Union News Co., New York, #477	c. 1911
320	Group of Prize Winners	V & Sons, #212589	1910
321	Mrs. Jay's Bar and Grill	Curt Teich, Chicago, #5A-H1673	c. 1950
322	Howard Johnson's	NPC Studios, Avon-By-the-Sea, N.J., #115032	c. 1960
323	Sand Statue, Asbury Park, N.J.	Tichnor, Boston, #131417	c. 1931
324	Hotel Carver	Dexter Press/Pointer Brothers, Clifton, N.J., #43776	c. 1960
325	Storyland Village	Dexter Press, West Nyack, N.Y., #86046	c. 1960
326	No Sunday Driving	Parlin Color Co., Toms River, N.J., #7982-B	c. 1960
327	Ocean Grove Auditorium	Curteich, Chicago, #6C-K1977	c. 1950
328	Avenue of Tents	Union News Co., New York, #599	c. 1920
329	St. Catherine's Catholic Church	Hugh C. Leighton Co., Portland, Maine	c. 1905
330	The World's Longest Bar	Dexter Press/Noumair Studios, Asbury Park, N.J., #63312	c. 1970
331	Sea Girt Lighthouse	Curteich, Chicago, #1C-H1578	c. 1940
332	Our House Tavern		c. 1940
333	Gateway to the Deserted Village	Hugh C. Leighton Co., Portland, Maine, #754	c. 1907
334	Molly Pitcher Well	Mayrose Co., Linden, N.J.	c. 1930
335	American Hotel and Restaurant	Curteich, Chicago, #D-9281	c. 1950
336	Hotel, Allentown, N.J.	J. Graham, Allentown, N.J.	c. 1915
337	Delicious Orchards	Dexter Press, West Nyack, N.Y., #92642-B	c. 1955
338	Garden State Arts Center	Custom Studios, Hackensack, N.J.	c. 1970
339	Point Pleasant Beach, N.J.	Parlin Color Co., Toms River, N.J., #S-71787	c. 1970
340	Point Pleasant, N.J., Grove and Pavilion	Union News Co., New York, #5793	c. 1911
341	Bay Head, N.J.	Dexter Press, West Nyack, N.Y., #DR-28065-B	c. 1968
342	Sunday Afternoon Bathers	Dick LaBonte	c. 1978
343	The John Wanamaker Commercial Institute	Tichnor, Boston, #121210	c. 1938
344	Sneak Box Race	Albertype Co., Brooklyn, N.Y.	c. 1923
345	Seaside Heights Carousel		c. 1905
346	Great Adventure		c. 1974

NO.	TITLE	PUBLISHER & NUMBER	DATE
347	Aerial View of Seaside Heights	#66174	c. 1944
348	Aerial View of Barnegat Light	Tichnor, Boston, #64386	c. 1949
349	Feeding Silk Worms		c. 1908
350	Pound Fishing Boat	Dexter Press, West Nyack, N.Y., #91169	c. 1950
351	Plant No. 3 of Cranberry Canners	Curt Teich, Chicago, #5A-H1984	c. 1940
352	America's Keswick	Continental Press, Philadelphia	c. 1930
353	The *Hindenburg*		c. 1936
354	St. Alexander Nevsky	Dexter Press, West Nyack, N.Y., #52830-B	c. 1960
355	A Close Game	Americhrome, New York, #M-7685	c. 1912
356	West Orange, N.J.	#3698	c. 1906
357	Garden State Post Card Club	#176276	1984
358	Young's Flip Flap Railway		1905
359	Hahnes & Co., Newark, N.J.		c. 1905
360	Railroad Avenue, Pedricktown, N.J.	P. P. Sweeten, Pedricktown, N.J., #1158	1905
361	Pusey & Jones Shipbuilding Co.		c. 1920
362	New Jersey	Scheller Co., Hackettstown, N.J., #57829	1962
363	Seidler's Beach	Landis & Alsop, Newark, N.J., #38972	c. 1920
364	Wm. H. Broadwell Commercial Photographer	Wm. H. Broadwell, Newark, N.J.	c. 1915
365	Lake Hopatcong	W. J. Harris, W. Pittston, Pa., and Lake Hopatcong, N.J.	c. 1906
366	Baptismal Service at Canton	Wm. J. S. Bradway, Hancock's Bridge, N.J.	c. 1905
367	Hightstown Railroad Station	Thorburn Studio, Hightstown, N.J.	c. 1907
368	Camden Post Office	Wm. B. Cooper, Medford, N.J.	c. 1910
369	Opera House, Cranford, N.J.	American News Co., New York, #11679	1910
370	Opera House Block Fire	Star Post Card Co., Plainfield, N.J.	1912
371	Colgate's Clock	Leighton & Valentine, New York, #207693	c. 1920
372	This Coupon Worth 20¢	#99-F5218	c. 1940
373	Cycling in the Good Old Days	Sherman Printing Co., Passaic, N.J.	1976
374	Weequahic Diner, Newark, N.J.	Harry Baumann, New York	c. 1920
375	Circus	Dexter Press, West Nyack, N.J., #77378	1960
376	Atlantic City Bathing Beauty		1907
377	Reward a Progressive School Board Man		1930
378	Marching through Jersey	Franz Huld, New York, #2	c. 1904
379	Tillie–Palace Amusements		1999
380	Eatontown Public School	Collotype, Elizabeth, N.J.	c. 1920
381	Pike Books	Rick Geary	2000

Index

About the Author

EATONTOWN PUBLIC SCHOOL, EATONTOWN, N.J.

Helen-Chantal Pike's first solo trip was the one-mile walk down Broad Street to her first day of kindergarten at the Fred G. Steelman School in Eatontown, New Jersey. To help teach her geography, a family friend sent chrome postcards of state capital buildings whenever he went on business trips. When she received an allowance, she spent her money buying postcards until she got her own camera.

After graduating from the Ranney School in Tinton Falls, she earned a B.A. in English and French from Principia College in Elsah, Illinois; a language certificate from La Sorbonne in Paris; and an M.S. degree from the Graduate School of Journalism at Columbia University.

Nostalgic for home while living in other places, she started collecting postcards of Asbury Park and other scenes from her childhood in the Garden State and from family vacations in New England. Then the day came when she returned home.

The rest is history.

380
Public School No. 1, built in 1907, was the first integrated school in town. It was later named for Fred G. Steelman, the district's longest-serving principal, who held the position from 1916 to 1940.

381
The art of cartoonist Rick Geary
of San Diego, California, is popular with postcard collectors

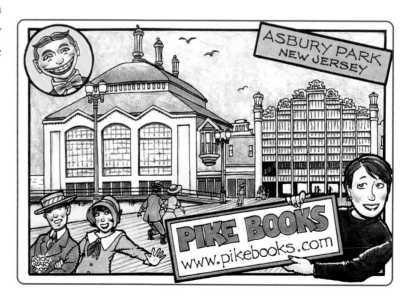